# TODAY WE

HARNESSING THE POWER OF TOTAL CONFIDENCE

Tyndale House Publishers, Inc.
CAROL STREAM, ILLINOIS

# ARE RICH

## Tim Sanders

Visit Tyndale's exciting Web site at www.tyndale.com.

Visit Tim's Web site at www.timsanders.com.

*TYNDALE* and Tyndale's quill logo are registered trademarks of Tyndale House Publishers, Inc.

*Today We Are Rich: Harnessing the Power of Total Confidence*

Designed by Ron Kaufmann

Edited by Susan Taylor

**Library of Congress Cataloging-in-Publication Data**

Sanders, Tim, date.
    Today we are rich : harnessing the power of total confidence / Tim Sanders.
        p. cm.
    Includes bibliographical references.
    ISBN 978-1-4143-3911-5 (hc)
1. Success. 2. Conduct of life. 3. Confidence. I. Title. II. Title: Harnessing the power of total confidence.
    BJ1611.2.S235 2011
    170'.44—dc22                                                          2010054344

Printed in the United States of America

17   16   15   14   13   12   11
7    6    5    4    3    2    1

*To Jacqueline—my muse, my rock, and*
*a source of abundance in my life.*

# Contents

# BILLYE'S LESSON I NEVER FORGOT

It was a typical sunny summer morning, and my grandmother and I were eating a breakfast of hot cereal, fresh biscuits, and Karo syrup. Through a freshly Spic-and-Span'd window, I spotted a stranger trudging through our wheat field toward the house. He was walking slowly, deliberately, with his head down. With each lumbering step, he appeared larger and larger.

Soon my grandmother noticed him too. She grabbed my hand, and together we made our way toward the field. We stopped in the peach orchard, just on the other side of the electric fence that surrounded the wheat field.

"Can I help you, sir?" my grandmother called out.

The man looked at us with a shy smile and replied, "I pray so, ma'am, I pray so." He took a long breath and continued: "My name is Clarence, and I need a day's work and a hot meal. I'm at my wit's end, ma'am, and I have no other options. But I am a good worker."

My grandmother sized him up—he was middle-aged and African American with salt-and-pepper hair and wore an ashy black suit with a yellowing white dress shirt underneath. He looked harmless, albeit shabby. She motioned for him to step over the fence and sit down with us on folding chairs around a card table in the orchard.

"I'm Billye," she said. "This here is my grandson, Tim. What's your story?"

"I've been walking for days, coming from my hometown, Dripping Springs, Oklahoma. I lost everything I owned in a swindle. I have nothing left but my winning smile, what's in this here pillowcase, and a few relatives who are willing to help me start over in Arizona."

He wiped his brow and said, "I just need some work, ma'am. I need someone to believe in me, if only for today."

Billye looked to the sky, as if seeking advice,

looked back at him, and then said, "I'll pay you ten dollars to work from right now till sundown. First, I need you to prune the tops of these peach trees. I can't reach them. Next, clean out the barn. And finally, if there's time left, you'll need to climb a ladder and touch up the trim on top of it."

Clarence hung his jacket on the limb of a peach tree and got right to work. So did I, walking around behind him as his pseudoforeman, commenting on his progress, and peppering him with all kinds of questions. He answered most of them with grunts. He finished the pruning in less than an hour and then started to clean out the barn. It was a dusty and herculean task.

Billye came out periodically to check up on us. Later she explained that she was making sure he wasn't leaning on his broom—a Southern phrase for "goofing off on the job."

At high noon she served lunch in the orchard on paper plates. It was a bounty: sliced hot dogs with ranch-style beans, mustard potato salad, Texas toast, and sweet tea. Clarence dug into his meal like he'd dug into his work that morning. His massive hands made his plastic fork look like a toothpick.

The more Clarence ate, the more conversational he became. He started to answer my questions more thoughtfully. He also started to dish me advice. He lowered his eyes and said, "I want to tell you something about your grandmother. She's special. She has faith!" He stopped to take a swig of his sweet iced tea.

"Miss Billye," he continued, "is an angel that God put on this earth to have faith in a stranger who needed someone to trust him. People like her make the world go round, boy. You understand?"

I nodded. I knew my grandmother was special. She had taken me into her home at a time when my own mother couldn't or wouldn't keep me. Billye loved me as if I were her own son, agreeing to raise me from the time I was four, even though she was getting on in years. She declared from the time I could walk that God had big plans for me. That's the kind of person she was—a big giver and believer in people.

"In the last few days I've had guns waved at me and dogs sicced on me," Clarence said. "I thought no one would give me a chance. But your grandmother did." He wiped his lips and summed up my lunch lesson: "See how happy she is? You will be too if you follow her example. You learn from your grandma's faith in people. Inherit some of her sweetness."

After lunch, Clarence really stepped up his efforts, as if energized by his meal. He cleaned out the entire barn, hauled off garbage, and painted all its trim.

Billye joined us at the end of the day to evaluate Clarence's work and pay him. She took a good look around, smiled, and said, "Clarence, you and I agreed on ten dollars for a good day's work. But today you gave a *great* day's work. You are a go-getter, and I appreciate that."

She pulled a worn twenty-dollar bill, a small fortune to us at the time, out of her clutch purse. She handed it to him and said, "For twice a good day's work, you deserve twice a good day's pay."

Wide-eyed, Clarence thanked her profusely. "You're an answer to prayer, ma'am."

"Speaking of prayer," she quickly replied, "would you pray with us before you leave?" Clarence eagerly obliged.

The three of us got down on our knees in the barnyard, just by the horse tie. Clarence went first. His prayer was brief but heartfelt. He thanked God for bringing him to this farm. He thanked God for Billye. He asked God to look over our farm and keep us safe and healthy.

Billye's prayer went on a bit longer, as I knew it would. Her prayers were always epic and usually made my knees go numb. She was, to quote Pastor Heck, "a prayer warrior." She started out by thanking God for Clarence's character and what it taught me about the value of hard work. And then, sobbing in joy, she thanked God for the opportunity to be a helpful part of his journey to Arizona, where he would make what she called "his great comeback." She asked God to put other Christian families in his path over the coming days.

With a final amen, she and I stood and dusted ourselves off. Clarence, however, stayed down on his knees, observing a lingering moment of silent prayer. As he knelt, we both noticed the holes in the soles of his shoes. They were the size of silver dollars, big enough to reveal his dirt-brown socks.

When Clarence stood up, Billye said, "After you put away the tools, come by the house on your way out. I have something you might want."

I helped Clarence clean up the tools, and when we got to the back door of the house, Billye was already there, beaming and holding up a brand-new pair of black wing-tip, go-to-Sunday-church shoes. I knew they had belonged to her deceased father, Tommie King, who had bought them a few months before he passed away. Billye had kept them in her bedroom closet "for a sunny day." (She never planned for rainy ones.)

"I hope these fit," she said, handing the shoes to Clarence. He quickly sat down on the porch swing to try them on. Slipping them on effortlessly and tying them, he smiled up at us and said, "They fit like they were made for me."

His eyes were glassy with tears. He shook Billye's hand and patted me on the head, then picked up his pillowcase of possessions and strutted off confidently toward the west, on his way to Arizona. I was in tears too, but I wiped them away so Clarence and Billye wouldn't see me bawling. I felt sorry for Clarence and, at the same time, elated at what we'd been able to do for him that day.

As we watched Clarence walk off into the sunset, Grandmother put her arm around me, squeezing me tightly to her side.

"Timothy," she said in a near whisper, her voice rising with each word, "today is a special day for us. Don't ever forget this feeling. Today we are rich!"

With the cadence of a minister, she repeated herself for emphasis:

"Today. We. Are. Rich."

◼

A few nights later Billye and I were having dinner at Burger Chef, a monthly treat. We split a chicken-fried-steak sandwich and a large bag of crinkle-cut fries and sipped Dr. Pepper over crushed ice.

There's just something about food that brings out philosophizing.

When we finished, as Billye gathered up the wrappers and napkins, I asked her, "When you said, 'We are rich,' the other day, what did you mean? You mean rich like Woody"—the owner of Turner's Department Store on Main Street—"or like Lane's dad?" (the attorney who drove the best car at church).

"Nope," she replied. "I meant that we have all we need, enough to share with Clarence. And because we were able to share, we're worth something. By being able and willing to give, we are rich."

The puzzled look on my face must have told her I didn't get it. She continued, "There's bank-account rich, and there's rich in spirit. The second kind is achieved when you make a difference. It's the forever kind of rich that no one can take away from you but you."

She held up her Dr. Pepper cup and tipped it so I could see inside. She had drunk about half of it.

"You see this?" she asked. "'Rich' means the cup's got enough in it to quench my thirst. More than enough. As far as I'm concerned, it's full, running over. If *you're* still thirsty, you can have some of mine. Get it?"

"But what if you get thirsty later?" I countered.

She took a little sip and then continued, unfazed by my question.

"I'm *con*fident," she stated, emphasizing the word's first syllable. "I believe in myself, all the people in my life, and even when everything else fails, God. Through all these beliefs, I know there is always more where this came from."

She had a twinkle in her eye, as if she knew she was teaching me something important. And she was. I understood that the key to being rich was the belief that there would always be more: the twenty-dollar bill, the soda pop, friends, family—anything.

I'll never forget the last thing she said as she pressed the buzzer for the carhop to pick up the tray: "Rich is a full cup and a light heart."

As we waited, her words hung in the air. I didn't quite know at that time the power of those words, but I could sense it: Billye wasn't just quoting truisms to me. She lived these truths because she had learned them the hard way. For Billye, life was a lesson in the ephemeral nature of being bank-account rich. She had come from a family of dirt farmers in Oklahoma who had saved just enough money to buy some land on the outskirts of Clovis on the eastern plains of New Mexico. Billye's father, Tommie King, worked hard, and everything he touched in Clovis turned to gold. He raised bumper crops, which allowed him to purchase even more land and a gas station/hotel.

Unlike the rest of Billye's high school classmates, she had her own car at seventeen. When she drove down Main Street, the boys on the football team would run beside the car and jump on the running boards to get a ride. Far away from the turmoil on Wall Street, her father was one of the few who had money to spend on machinery, fertilizer, and manpower.

Then, during the 1940s, Tommie suffered a setback. For more than a decade, he'd been sending most of his money back to Oklahoma, where a pair of cousins had a bank. As it turned out, they were swindlers. Virtually overnight the Kings became land rich and cash poor.

By the 1960s, my grandmother Billye Coffman, now married to a retired air force officer, had earned it all back through hard work. She had a prosperous farm and a hair salon that did a brisk business.

A few years later, she lost it all again. Lloyd, her husband, poisoned her reputation at the air base, where most of her clients lived. He ran up credit all over town, then told banker friends that Billye was crazy. When he left town, all she had was the stuff in the house. She was land rich and cash poor again.

But through these highs and lows, Billye learned a valuable life lesson: You can't control your material wealth, but by cultivating a strong sense of confidence, you *can* control your attitude about whether there's enough to go around.

Billye's charity toward Clarence was a part of her mental exercise program to cultivate her sense of confidence and faith. Even though that twenty-dollar bill was gone, we were still having our monthly burgers and getting by just fine.

As Billye turned the ignition switch on her Buick Electra, she summed up the idea: "Being rich is a decision that stems from a sense of *con*fidence. It's right up here," she said, tapping her forefinger on the side of her head. "Listen to me: Confidence is rocket fuel." She revved the car's engine for emphasis. "It'll fill you up and make you believe there will be enough of what you need. The other day with Clarence was your first lesson in abundant living."

At that exact moment I realized that Clarence was right about one thing: I'd be a smart kid to study my grandmother and be like her. He was wrong about her being an angel, though. She was my confidence teacher. A tingle crawled up the back of my neck as it occurred to me that *Clarence* had been the angel, put in our field that day to teach me a lesson about life. I didn't realize at the time that it was a lesson I would stray from but never forget.

**PART 1**

# The Case for Confidence

# 1

# SIDEWAYS YEARS

I first met Eric Goldhart in 1997.[1] With his toned physique and strong, confident demeanor, he was known as a "rock star" at his company. As the top producer and de facto sales leader at his dot-com start-up in Dallas, Eric possessed a charismatic let-me-lead-you personality that could convince even the most conservative staffing professionals to spend money with his Internet company. Eternally optimistic, Eric had a ready answer for any prospect's objection. In fact, he loved skeptical clients or tough audiences because he saw them not as obstacles but as opportunities.

Eric and I met when I was asked to give a presentation at his company's annual sales-awards dinner. We hit it off immediately because we had a lot in common: We'd both been raised by our grandmothers. We liked to read the same types of books. We'd both been successful in our fields and had similar dreams of running our own companies someday.

In the months that followed, we spun it up over long lunches, exchanging tips and dreaming about when we would eventually make it big in the business world. And the next year I wasn't surprised to hear that Eric had been recruited by a Seattle-based leasing company as the western regional vice president of sales. As far as I knew, Eric was well on his way to running Microsoft someday.

I didn't hear from Eric again until early 2002, when an e-mail from him arrived, asking me for a few minutes on the phone. I could tell by the tone of his e-mail that something was very wrong. This was not the "rock star" I once knew. This was someone who had lost his way and needed help. I called him that weekend, and we talked for over an hour as he laid out his problem in detail.

Since 2001, the dot-com industry had been under fire from Wall Street, and Eric's region, which stretched from Silicon Valley to Seattle, had been the hardest hit. Each week start-ups of all types were running out of cash and shuttering their businesses, breaking leases, and selling cubicles and computers for pennies on the dollar.

The mood in the industry was darker than the weather, and just as depressing. As survivor companies implemented massive layoffs, Eric found himself pummeled from every side by messages of fear and insecurity. When he worked out at the gym, talking heads on cable television spelled out all the ways the coming recession would likely unfold. Newspapers ran headlines hysterically predicting the end of the Internet era. Even Eric's coworkers were growing increasingly concerned and wondering when the hammer would drop on them, too.

Even though Eric was a long-standing optimist, he couldn't resist the fear chatter. Against his better judgment, he read, listened to, and viewed these scare-lines like drivers who can't look away from a car-crash scene. Before long, his positive outlook evaporated. He began to question his ability and commitment and to wonder whether he had enough talent and drive to survive the impending economic storm. He even started to feel guilty for taking downtime or enjoying himself, attributing the root of the dot-com industry's failures to an overabundance of fun.

Suffering from a shortage of confidence, Eric became doubtful about his own company's chances of survival, even though senior management was holding to a more positive, wait-and-see attitude. Deciding to take on this fight himself, Eric hunkered down and told himself that it was up to him to come up with instant sales solutions.

He stopped going to the gym because he felt guilty when he wasn't working. Leaving work at six in the evening felt morally wrong—inasmuch as the ship was presumably sinking—so he stayed late at the office, missing dinner with his wife and two toddlers.

Even when he was at home, his mind stayed in overdrive mode. He snapped at his wife and kids, locked himself away in the den with his computer, and sat glued to the cable news channels for hours at a time. He stopped having morning devotions—they seemed insipid in the face of reality—and attending church with his family. The only thing that mattered was finding some way out of the mess in which he found himself.

Trapped in an emotional spin cycle and sleeping fitfully at best, Eric started chewing his fingernails and developed puffy circles under his eyes. At work, his productivity plummeted faster than the stock market. He wasted hours rereading the same set of bad numbers from a variety of sources. He pored over an endless supply of downward projections and combed the Internet for more bad news on the horizon.

For every minute Eric worked, he worried for ten. And his outlook was contagious. He badgered his salespeople to work harder because times were apocalyptic. In meetings, he filled his coworkers with personal doubts and fears, which led to a swift decline in personal productivity on their part. Customer sales calls often ended up with a gloom-and-doom session that left all parties worse off than when they started.

At the end of the year, Eric's boss gave him a lukewarm annual review and a warning: "Get your groove back, or I'll have to replace you." Eric had never been demoted or fired in his young career, and now he was on the brink of both.

At this point, Eric was running on empty. He was in a full-blown personal recession. He was shrinking as a person, drinking far too much, and chasing away everyone in his life. He knew things had to change, and on New Year's Eve he made a resolution: *I'm going to get help, and I'm going to make a comeback.*

That's when he wrote to me.

As I listened to Eric talk on the phone that afternoon, I had to admit that his story sounded eerily familiar. He described 2001 as a year he failed to move forward in any part of his life; in other words, he had experienced his first "sideways" year. At that point, I knew I could help him. He'd only had one of those years. I'd had fifteen of them in a row. My sideways years had stretched from my early twenties to my midthirties, and I was proof positive that you can fill your tank back up and come roaring back.

I knew that the way for me to help Eric was to share my story with him, one that I'd always been reluctant to tell.

It was late summer 1981, and I was out for a spin west of town in my candy-apple-red Pontiac Astre, rocking out to an eight-track tape of the band Yes on my new car stereo. The song "Close to the Edge" was playing, and I was singing along at the top of my lungs when I noticed flashing headlights in my rearview mirror. When I pulled over, I recognized my uncle Jim's black Monte Carlo rolling up behind me. We got out of our cars, and when he approached me, he put his hand on my shoulder and said with a heavy sigh, "I don't know how else to say this. Your father's been murdered, Tim. I'm so sorry."

I stood there on the side of the road in shock, mumbling the words back to him, "My father's been murdered. . . ."

As I followed Jim back to the house, a slide show of times with Dad played in my mind. I could smell his aftershave—he always wore Brut—and feel his whiskers pressing against my cheek as he hugged me. Fighting tears, I tried to distract myself by changing tapes in the car, only to hear Diana Ross and the Supremes sing "Someday We'll Be Together." I had to keep my eyes glued to Jim's taillights for the rest of the way home to avoid driving off the road.

Even though I had spent only a week or so with my dad each summer when I was growing up, he had made a big impression on me. He had been forced to give me up twice: first to his wife (my mom) and then later to his own mother (Billye) when my mom decided she couldn't raise me. My dad had a jack-of-all-trades career and a big-city lifestyle, and he knew I would be better off with Billye. Even though we were apart, he called me often, mostly to tell me how much he loved me.

The week before his death, my father, Tom Sanders, had accepted a writing position with a television production company in Los Angeles, the same city where I was attending college. It was the first time we would be living in the same city, and I had been looking forward to getting to know him better. He was funny, smart, and sophisticated and had always been one of my biggest fans.

Now, it was all gone. Our reunion seemed to have been canceled by fate.

When I got home, Billye was there, surrounded by friends and family. She knew I would be a wreck, so when she saw me come through the front door, she stood up and extended her arms toward me. She was ready to comfort me, as she always did during my difficult moments. Billye had always been my rock. Her solid faith and serene confidence had inspired me to achieve so much during high school and my first two years in college.

For years Billye had taught me confidence lessons as I sat perched on the edge of the bathtub. While she shaped her beehive hairdo, she shared tips I could employ the next day. Her lessons had paid off in my life. I went from being labeled a "discipline problem" and being placed in the local special-education program in second grade to returning to public school and making the honor roll in sixth grade, in spite of being called "Short Bus Sanders" by the other kids. By my senior year of high school, I was on a roll: class president and state champion in debate. Just a few months before my dad's death, I had received a debate scholarship to finish college at a prestigious school on the West Coast, after winning several junior college national championships. Yes, Billye's hard-won life lessons on confidence had turned my life around.

Yet on that day, something inside me snapped. As Billye tried to get me to join her prayer circle of family and friends, I snarled, "Why would God do this to him? Why would he do this to me?" She was crestfallen and hurt. She didn't have the energy to pursue me. All she could do was bow her head and begin to pray.

Billye's words about a loving God didn't make sense to me anymore. In an instant my faith had been shattered. Suddenly, I no longer trusted anyone. Since all of Billye's principles were based, in some part, on her faith, her teachings no longer had the ring of truth to me.

When I left Clovis to move to California later that month, rejecting everything Billye had taught over the years about how to live life, I didn't take a single book from the family library with me, even though Billye offered them all. I didn't even bring my Bible.

As I went through the motions of my junior year in college at Loyola Marymount University, everything was different. I no longer cared about earning good grades or making something of myself. I skipped classes, took shortcuts in my research, and coasted along, just getting by with what little confidence I had leftover from the previous years.

My sideways years had begun.

When I moved to Tucson to attend graduate school, my attitude shifted from a simple lack of faith and trust to one of full-blown negativity. I decided that my championship years as a debater had been little more than dumb luck, and I figured I'd better take whatever I could get in terms of a job. When I landed a consulting position at Hughes Aircraft, I again assumed it was a fluke. Since I couldn't imagine ever being successful in business, I didn't take the position seriously.

Instead, pursuing my passion for music, I joined a local band and settled into a month-to-month lifestyle that eventually left me in a broken-down school bus in an RV park just east of Dallas, Texas.

A few years later, I met Jacqueline, who became the love of my life. I was a mess at the time, but she saw something beneath my black rocker clothes and penchant for pessimism. Her son, Anthony, was four years old at the time, and I fell in love with him, too. Still, I didn't have the confidence or ambition to strive for more than living paycheck to paycheck.

I found a sales job in the cable television business that leveraged my gift of gab. And even though I made good money, I always found a way to sabotage my path toward management. I was earning a solid income, but I still wasn't happy. I had no goals other than to be discovered one day by a record mogul and stop working for "the man."

By the spring of 1996, I was near the breaking point. I quit my job, cashed in my 401(k), and devoted my energy to getting a record deal—even though I knew deep down that it was a next-to-impossible feat. I took odd jobs to help with the rent, and we ate on the tips that Jacqueline made as a hairstylist. Each day I became more disappointed in myself, and one afternoon while driving home, I had a sudden impulse to jerk the car's steering wheel to the right and drive full speed into the concrete freeway barrier. The compulsion was so strong that I had to pull the car over and stop until I regained my composure. It wasn't the first time such a dark thought had crossed my mind that year. When I told Jacqueline about it that night, I cried uncontrollably, shaking in her arms as she tried to console me.

I was far away from the wide-eyed kid Billye had taught to love life and achieve great things. I knew I needed to find a way out of my sideways years, even if it meant going backward—back to a time and place where life made sense.

# 2

# THE AWAKENING

Eric and I had our second coaching phone call the week of Valentine's Day 2002. I began our conversation with a question: "What are you *not* doing today that you *were* doing when I first met you?"

"I'm not sure what you mean," Eric said, laughing nervously.

"What investments in yourself and others are you no longer making?" I asked. "What daily or weekly practices for a better *you* have fallen by the wayside?"

If Eric could answer these questions, I knew he could pull himself out of his negativity and get back on track. There was power in these words. How did I know? I was living proof. Billye had asked these exact questions of me in 1996, just months after I had nearly rammed my car into a concrete wall.

I had been emotionally disconnected from Billye ever since my dad's death. In my mind, I wasn't that little kid sitting on the edge of the bathtub anymore, listening to her spout life lessons. I'd gone off to college in Los Angeles and learned how to doubt. Now I was "worldly."

But when dark thoughts of worthlessness and suicide began to be part of my daily routine, I knew it was time for me to reconnect with my rock in life—Billye. During the Thanksgiving holiday, Jacqueline and I flew to Lubbock and rented a car to drive to Clovis. We bought a disposable camera at the local Walgreens, and I gave Jacqueline a tour of my hometown, taking pictures of places and things that had meant something to me when I was growing up: the wheat farm, the cemetery where my father was buried, the high school I attended. Billye encouraged me to take pictures of my debate trophy collection in my bedroom, which she had left proudly on display, but I refused.

"That was a hundred years ago," I snapped. I had little confidence of ever returning to the glory days of my earlier years. To me, those types of achievements would remain in the distant past forever.

Once we were back in Dallas, I turned in the camera for developing and got back twenty or so prints. As I flipped through the photos—snapshots of the farm, Billye sitting at the kitchen table, the cemetery where my dad was buried—the last picture in the stack nearly stopped my heart. It was a picture of the water tower in Sudan, Texas—the very spot where Billye took final delivery of me after my mom had abandoned me in a hotel. It wasn't the first time my hapless mom had misplaced me, but in Billye's eyes, it would be the last.

As I stared at that photo, it dawned on me that it couldn't have been a worse time for Billye to adopt a child. In addition to supporting me, she was also responsible for her eighty-five-year-old mother, Hattie. Billye's twenty-year marriage had just broken up, the bank accounts were dry, and her credit had been extended to the breaking point.

My mind floated back to the hot summer day when two imposing repo men had forced their way into our kitchen. Within minutes, our refrigerator and stove were loaded into a white truck, and our kitchen sat empty. That was the first time I ever saw Billye cry.

But it didn't take her long to shake herself off.

After locking herself in the bathroom for a couple of hours, Billye came out and announced that we would be just fine. Ever industrious, she talked to neighbors and church members, trading haircuts and bookkeeping for used appliances until our kitchen was back in working order—even though nothing matched.

Billye had made the decision to claim me in spite of the sacrifices it would require, and it was that choice that turned an unwanted and abandoned little boy into someone who felt valued and cherished. As I stared at the grainy image of that water tower, a familiar tingle crawled down the back of my neck. A quiet voice reasoned that if Billye could lose everything and still come out on top, I could get over my dad being taken away from me. For me, the water tower was symbolic of hope: Anybody's story can start over again and, through the love of others, have a happy ending.

That night, I opened up a book Billye had given me: *Think and Grow Rich*. It was one of her most cherished books in the family library, handed down by her father, Tommie King. Flipping to a random page, I found these words to be a cool drink to my soul: "Go back into your yesterdays, at times, and bathe your mind in the beautiful memories of past love. It will soften the influence of the present worries and annoyances. It will give you a source of escape from the unpleasant realities of life and maybe—who knows?—your mind will yield to you, during this temporary retreat into the world of . . . plans which may change the entire financial or spiritual status of your life."[1]

I looked across the bed at my wife, Jacqueline, who always believed in me and was willing to wait for me to grow into my potential. I thought of our son, Anthony, snoozing in the next room, a precious young man who deserved a powerful father. I snapped the book closed, blinked back tears, and let the water-tower moment linger in my mind as sleep descended on me.

The next day I called Billye during my lunch hour.

"I'm ready to go back in time," I offered up, "to the lessons you taught me, the books you told me to read, and the daily do's you gave me. I've been terrible to everyone, and I've got no one to hold accountable for it but myself."

"Hmm," she replied. "Sounds like your heart is tender and your mind is open."

"Jacqueline and Anthony deserve better," I continued. "They deserve a champion."

"Let me ask you a few questions," she said, surprising me that she wasn't immediately launching into a sermonette.

"What are you *not* doing these days that you *were* doing during your senior year in high school and your early days in college?" she asked, like a rural-route Socrates.

I thought back to the lessons she had taught me during my teen years, the habits she had helped me develop, and the principles upon which I had built my success. They were simple ideas, really, but at the same time, deep and powerful: Feed Your Mind Good Stuff, Exercise Your Gratitude Muscle, Prepare Yourself.

I ticked off a list of daily rituals that were no longer part of my routine: reading for the good of my soul, doing things to improve my personal résumé every year, volunteering, taking care of my body.

Billye listened carefully and then confirmed that I was on the right track.

"You know what to do," she said, "because I taught you. Your life lacks the daily practices you once had. You've taken your faith and your spiritual practices for granted. It's time to go back to what works—back to the basics. And it starts with rereading the masters: James Allen, Dr. Norman Vincent Peale, Napoleon Hill, Dale Carnegie, Claude Bristol, and Maxwell Maltz."

My mind swirled with excitement as we talked.

I *knew* how to do this! I had simply allowed the uncertainties of life to get in the way of doing what I needed to do.

"It all starts today," I said as I wrapped up our call. "Your Timothy is back among the living, Mom." Billye always wanted me to call her Mom, as she'd raised me as one of her own. When I did, she'd get that sparkle of pleasure in her voice.

"Today we are rich!" she crowed.

And since that day, I've never been poor.

# 3

# THE GOOD LOOP

Billye's question on that lunch-hour phone call set me on a new, exciting path. I went from being an entry-level salesperson at a start-up multimedia business to an executive at Yahoo! in fewer than four years. And then, suddenly, I got a book deal, which launched me into new speaking opportunities. And it all started with getting back to the basic principles of living that Billye had taught me when I was a kid. Following the principles of confidence had definitely put me in a good loop.

So when I asked the same question of Eric on that Valentine's Day, I knew from experience that the question contained a lot of power.

"What are you *not* doing today that you *were* doing when I first met you?"

At first, Eric's answer was flippant: "Having fun and being high on life."

But when I countered, "No, Eric, I mean, what investments in yourself and others are you no longer making? What daily or weekly practices for a better *you* have fallen by the wayside?" He got more circumspect about what he had let go of: "Reading business books. I've definitely lost the luxury of reading about the future. . . . Giving, sharing, teaching, coaching, pitching in, networking, and helping my customers succeed. I'm in survival mode, dude."

My phone call with Eric got him thinking about all the habits he had given up during the dot-com crash. He had let his uncertainty about the future knock his entire life out of whack. Billye had always warned me about that: "Uncertainty is a spiritual enemy that will siphon out your rocket fuel. It turns go-getters into giver-uppers." As I hung up the phone after talking to Eric, I wondered whether Billye's question would make a difference in his life as it had in mine.

On the first Monday in 2003, I got my answer. Eric sat down at his laptop to tap out an update for me on his progress. The tone of the note signaled right away that he was in a good place emotionally and spiritually. The subject line said it all: *I'm baaaack!*

He explained how he'd thought about my questions and changed his daily media diet from "grist to good stuff." He popped CDs of great books into his car every day on his long commute, starting with *Good to Great* by Jim Collins. Instead of combing through the *Financial Times* every morning, he read inspiring devotionals. Instead of watching cable television news, he tuned in to his kids playing with the family dog. He saw his outlook improve almost immediately. "You have no idea what a difference a year makes! I changed what went into my noggin, what came out of my mouth, and what's come into my life!" Eric was in a good loop, thanks to Billye's principles of confidence. His thoughts led to positive actions. They created positive results in his life, which encouraged him to continue in his good loop. That's how it works.

Again and again I've noticed in other people's lives the same experience Eric and I have had.

Unless you are living the principles of confidence fully, suffering or uncertainty can shake up your belief in others—or even in God. Eric faced adversity, and I experienced a personal tragedy. Eric lost self-confidence first, and then eventually trust and faith. I had lost faith first, and then eventually trust in others and my own self-confidence. We had both slipped into a negative loop, but the result was the same: sideways years. Both Eric and I drifted during our times of crisis because we had underestimated the importance of maintaining our confidence with life-giving habits.

Billye knew from experience the crucial link between confidence and achievement, but multiple studies have confirmed that when you *believe* you'll be successful, you achieve a calmness that improves your ability to slow life's game down and see things more clearly. As Dr. Peale says, when you conquer worry, you can "relax for easy power."[1]

Countless studies pioneered by Dr. Albert Bandura document this clarity gain in students who believe they are prepared for a test and confident in their abilities to ace it. When you think you'll get an A, the test is an opportunity to shine, not a daunting task. Your relaxed mind is able to add two plus two and come up with four, in contrast to the nervous mind, which can be fraught with basic errors in math, logic, reason, and judgment. A modern study conducted at Goldsmiths University of London concluded that confidence is just as important as one's IQ in a testing environment. Think of it this way: Your mind is either clear or cluttered with negative thoughts. Self-confidence is a purifier of sorts that reduces the chatter in your head and allows you to fall into a state of flow. You have likely felt this during an activity you consider yourself very good at. You don't really have to think about what you're doing; you just do it.

Many people I've talked to point out how they are more influenced by people's credentials than by their perspectives, but I think that's wishful thinking on their parts. Carnegie Mellon University professor Don A. Moore researched this proposition and through a carefully crafted experiment found that humans are more likely to accept a person's advice because of the communicator's level of certainty than because of his or her track record or résumé. Show me someone who lights up a room, commands respect, and charms everyone, and I'll point out the underlying energy that makes it all possible: confidence.

◼

In the years following my conversation with Billye, and then with Eric, I became convinced of my next assignment: to inspire a new generation to model total confidence at a time when fear was spreading like a virus.[2] Once again, I started by going back to the source of those lessons—Billye.

What follows in part 2 are seven principles distilled from Billye's life and teachings. I have tested them by studying the research on motivation and by talking to master motivational experts. These principles will change your life. I know because they have turned my own life around twice—first when they launched me into a good loop in my high school years, and second when they powered me out of my sideways years in my thirties. They will have an immediate impact on your perspective, and you'll be able to measure that impact through your increased performance. You'll sleep better, be happier, and do the world more good than you did before you learned them. Eventually, life will start spinning in a good loop for you as it did for Eric and for me. Some of the principles will be consistent with what you've been raised to believe. Others might be different—even difficult to swallow—but that has no bearing on their effectiveness.

Each of the following chapters contains a principle followed by a set of practices designed to improve your outlook in two areas: your circumstances and the participants (including you) who will be a part of your new future. I'm not going to try to make this sound easy. These principles require a lot of work. You'll have to invest time and energy to live by them, and you'll likely need some patience to stick with them. But my promise to you is that if you do, you will lead a life of consistent achievement—a life that continues to move forward, which can only create goodness for everyone around you. A life in which a set of principles works to keep you on track, regardless of whatever comes along.

If you bought this book because you have struggled recently and want your "swagger" back, then this is your water-tower moment, a time for renewal. If you are a confident person who wants to stay confident, this is a way to keep yourself moving forward. The secret to renewal and true confidence is simple: Get back to the basics.

# PART 2

# The Principles of Total Confidence

**4**

# FEED YOUR MIND GOOD STUFF

Billye got up with the chickens at the crack of dawn and yet kept bankers' hours. What did she do during the hours in between? She fed her mind good stuff.

During my childhood, I observed her morning routine hundreds of times. When she got out of bed, she would walk out on her patio and slowly stretch. Then she'd sit down in her easy chair in the living room and read the Bible for about fifteen minutes. After pouring her first cup of coffee, she'd read a book, a devotional, or the latest edition of *The Midnight Cry* or *Guideposts*. Meanwhile, the *Clovis News Journal*, the town's local paper, would sit on the front porch with the rubber band still on it. After a half hour or so of mindful reading, Billye would make notes in her journal, mostly insights from the morning's study.

On many mornings, she followed her reading with a phone call to one of her closest friends, who followed a similar morning mind practice. They talked about what they had read or thought about and often giggled, too. Billye's final piece of the prework morning was a long prayer as she knelt in front of her easy chair. Afterward, she'd get up, eat breakfast, and get ready for a hard day's work.

Billye never watched television during the day. When she occasionally tuned in to the news, she trusted only a few news sources, such as Walter Cronkite or Edward R. Murrow. "The rest of them," she'd say, "are scare merchants, selling soap by dirtying our minds." She watched only movies or television programs that had positive themes and avoided violence or vulgarity with the switch of a channel. To her, the *R* in an R rating stood for "rubbish."

Billye was just as judicious in her response to what others tried to put in her head. She avoided "gossip snipes" as if they had an infectious disease. She even dumped negative-minded friends after one too many offenses. When one of the ladies at our church asked her why a Christian woman would quit friends over the words they used, Billye would paraphrase Dr. Norman Vincent Peale from *The Power of Positive Thinking*: "What comes out of the mind is what you put in the mind. You must feed your mind like you feed your body."

Her positive-intake plan wasn't selfish—it was purposeful. The filter she put on what or whom she listened to wasn't prud*ish*—it was prud*ent*. The secret to positive thinking, she had learned, lies in consuming the right mind food. From waking thoughts to the edge of sleep, she fed her mind mostly good stuff.

Rick, a friend of mine from my Yahoo! days, had a different morning routine—one much more familiar to many of us. When he woke up—usually springing out of bed right after he slapped his alarm off—he fired up the coffee pot and booted his laptop. He downloaded his e-mails, many of which had come in earlier that morning from the East Coast. He'd answer a few, fill his coffee cup, and weed-whack through the rest. After that, he'd hit the home page of Yahoo!, *The Huffington Post*, and a few blogs he followed, and then graze. Often he'd get sucked into a social-networking site such as Facebook or Twitter until he realized that he was running late for work.

As he drove to work, he listened to morning talk radio, much of it either crude or political. While he waited at stoplights, he checked his e-mail on his phone or answered texts from coworkers. At lunch, he worked out in the gym while watching CNBC and then pored over the newspaper while he ate. In the evening, he watched the evening news over dinner and, following that, a slew of reality shows or sitcoms. After dinner he'd surf the Web for an hour, answer any e-mails he'd received since he left work, and then try to get some sleep before the alarm went off again the next morning.

When I met with Rick, he complained that he was becoming increasingly depressed. The first thing I asked him to do was describe his "information-intake day," and after he did, in my best imitation of Dr. Phil McGraw, I asked him, "How's that working for you?"

Rick's problem was his mind diet. It wasn't thoughtful, and it didn't take his perspective into account. And that's ironic because Rick is a health nut. He doesn't eat refined sugars, red meat, processed foods, or non-organic fruit and vegetables. He scrutinizes menus for details about ingredients and presses servers for nutritional information about items he's considering. When it comes to mind food, however, he piles it on like rock candy and double cheeseburgers.

When I shared with him the mind diet I'm about

to share with you, it led to a radical change in Rick's attitude and level of confidence. When he realized that his mind "ate," just as his body did, with good or bad results, he changed his information lifestyle, got some new friends, and took back his point of view.

You should be as careful about what you put into your mind as about what you put into your mouth. Your mind is a machine. When you ingest a piece of information, your mind goes to work, chewing on it, digesting it, and then converting it into a thought. When good stuff goes into your mind, good thoughts emerge. People who maintain purposeful mind diets of positive stimuli think healthy thoughts.

The reason it is so important to feed your mind good stuff is that the resulting thoughts determine your success or failure, your happiness or misery, and most important, the circumstances of your life. Those who do not have a diet plan for their minds are subject to their worst memories and the world's constant fear chatter—and those result in disturbing thought patterns.

> **You should be as careful about what you put into your mind as you are about what you put into your mouth.**

That's essentially the premise behind Napoleon

Hill's *Think and Grow Rich*: "Every man is what he is, because of the *dominating thoughts* which he permits to occupy his mind. . . . We are what we are, because of the vibrations of thought which we pick up and register, through the stimuli of our daily environment."[1]

And Hill wasn't the only one to write about the importance of our thoughts. James Allen wrote his groundbreaking book *As a Man Thinketh* in 1903, with Proverbs 23:7 as its premise: "As he thinketh in his heart, so is he" (KJV). The premise of his book was simple, yet profound: "Good thoughts bear good fruit; bad thoughts bear bad fruit."

In *The Magic of Believing*, Claude Bristol revealed that we have two minds: the conscious mind and the subconscious mind.[2] Almost seventy years of psychological research since the book was published support his hypothesis. Thoughts become reality because of our subconscious mind, which produces our feelings, instincts, and actions.

The conscious mind is the always-on machine that reacts to stimuli and steers the subconscious mind. It's smaller, designed to quickly analyze and interpret. The subconscious mind is the larger of the two, a massive cerebral hard drive that stores every observation, experience, or interaction in your life.

By design, your conscious mind stores far less in order to preserve operating room for interpreting fresh stimuli.

Trying unsuccessfully to recall a name, a band, a movie, or a book when it's just on the tip of your tongue likely drives you crazy. Eventually, sometimes much later, the word or phrase you seek comes to you, almost like magic, and you feel an incredible sense of relief. You're unstuck! That's the work of the subconscious mind, retrieving the information from the vault. You hadn't really forgotten the information; you had just sent it to your subconscious mind to free up room in the conscious mind for taking in new information.

The subconscious isn't just a mass storage device either. Maxwell Maltz wrote that it's also the creative mechanism that generates your basic instincts, intuitions, actions, and reactions. Thoughts create beliefs in the conscious mind; once sent to the subconscious, those beliefs become feelings and actions.[3]

If your subconscious computes that you will likely succeed at something, it brings all your powers to bear to make it come true. If it computes that you'll fail, it will generate behavior to make that come true—that's what it means to be self-destructive.

Your thoughts also shape how others see you, react

to you, and further inform your self-image. Your thoughts, and their resulting emotions, leak out for others to decode via their subconscious minds, which run their nervous systems. That is why your body language betrays your spoken words. It's also why you can suffer a negative outburst that reveals your true feelings—no matter how much you tell your conscious mind to maintain self-control.

James Allen put it best when he wrote, "We may imagine that thought can be kept secret, but it cannot; it rapidly crystallizes into habit, and habit solidifies into circumstance."[4] You think, you act, and your actions create a series of events that shape your day-to-day life.

Think about a time when you were in a mind funk. The more you thought about how you felt, the more upset you became. When you were with friends, you were a ticking time bomb of emotions. You tried to suppress them, but you almost always failed and ended up saying something you wish you hadn't.

Even if you can keep your mouth zipped, your body language betrays you. You fold your arms, roll your eyes, or fidget nervously. Other people interpret your actions as hostile, and they distance themselves from you or return your negativity with their own hostility. This only makes you feel worse, and you drop into a vicious cycle of bad-thought-driven behavior.

Finally, thoughts also have an impact on your physical health. The subconscious mind tells the body what to do, how to feel, and which chemicals to create. When the subconscious mind converts a negative thought into fear and stress, the body produces the stress hormone cortisol. Over time, production of this hormone can lead to heart disease and digestive issues.[5]

And although modern science has made great progress in understanding how emotional stress affects physical health, writers were already seeing a connection decades ago. Maxwell Maltz humorously pointed out, "Someone had said that the greatest cause of ulcers is mountain-climbing over molehills."[6] And Dr. Peale wrote, "Many people suffer poor health not because of what they eat but from what is eating them."[7] The problem with so many people I encounter who complain of aches and pains is that they have indigestion of the soul.

In my personal experience, positive thinking is the key to health. I believe my own health is shaped by my thoughts the way a sculpture is shaped by its creator. I am very careful about my mind diet and consider myself a healthy-thought nut.

## KEEP A MIND FOOD JOURNAL

Many nutritionists and weight-loss professionals say that the first step in any diet program is to take inventory of what you are taking into your body. In 2002, I decided that I needed to lose weight and get in shape. Over a four-year period, while traveling the world for business, I had been eating too much fattening comfort food, and as a result, I had expanded my waistline by six inches! My "spider belly" looked funky on my small frame, and I realized that I needed to change my ways.

When I started on my plan of action, my diet consultant's first piece of advice was to write down everything I ate. *Everything.* In a journal I logged every item I put in my mouth. When I reviewed it a few weeks later, I was horrified. The vast majority of what I had recorded was garbage: refined sugars, processed foods, and simple carbs. No wonder I had been putting on pounds! Keeping that journal was a powerful first step, and it helped me to shave forty pounds and four inches off my waistline in less than two years.

Now here's an exercise for you: For the next few weeks, log everything you are reading, listening to, or watching. If you want to get the most out of this book, purchase a small journal you can carry with you. It will be useful for your mind diet as well as for other exercises I'll give you later. Record the source, the author (if applicable), and the tone (positive, helpful, neutral, negative) of everything you take into your mind. Next to each entry, note how much time you spent on it. The same goes for people you spend time with. Log their names, their tone, and how much time you spent with them. Also—and this is important in the age we live in—note how much time you spend on the Internet on activities not related to work. Now, circle all the negative or useless information and influences you've "consumed," and highlight all the positive or helpful ones. Quickly scan your entire journal to form an initial impression of your total intake, positive or negative. If you find many more circles than highlighted items, you need to focus your efforts on eliminating those "foods" from your mind diet. The longer you do this, the more aware of your mind diet you'll be, and the more control you'll have over it. For many people, the early results will be alarming, just as much as my food diet journal was for me!

## FILTER OUT THE NEGATIVE

Now that you've seen just what your mind diet consists of, you are ready to eliminate junk mind food and negative influences from your diet. They are toxins and fillers that cannot coexist with positive information. They often expand and squeeze out any good stuff you've downloaded into your mind.

Think of curiosity as the driver of your news-of-the-weird cravings. In an attempt to "keep up" with what's going on in the world, you can't help but click on a link to the latest news on Lindsay Lohan or on the latest virus that's going to infect the world. But much like I had to do in my weight-loss program, you'll have to conquer your cravings through willpower.

I believe that most television news coverage is not intended to inform you—it is designed to glue you to it so you'll watch the ads and buy the products sold. Longtime broadcast journalist Ted Koppel wrote that to be effective, a news feature must be a "ladle dropper," meaning that it requires Mom to drop her ladle in the soup when she hears the headline and run to the TV to pay attention to the gory details.[8] That's why positive stories don't usually drive ratings. They don't scare us enough to hold our attention. Watch the local television news every night, and you'll hear about car crashes, murders, political scandals, sports, and the weather (which you can gather in a minute at weather.com).

Avoid gossip the way you would the flu. It's a socially acceptable form of pornography that is hurtful. Other people's misfortunes should never be a source of entertainment. When you encounter a Web site, broadcast program, or magazine that peddles gossip, stop reading or watching it immediately. Beware of celebrity-focused publications. They promote voyeurism, a particularly cruel form of media.

When it comes to Internet usage, be purposeful. Don't just graze, clicking around until something grabs your attention. You'll eventually stumble onto a disturbing news item. In Las Vegas, the casinos have a rule that works: Keep the bettors at the table long enough, and they will always lose. If you insist on reading around the daily Web, follow Maxwell Maltz's rule of thumb: "Glance at negatives, but focus on positives."[9]

Next, filter out negative people and their nasty attitudes. They are often more credible to you than the media and can produce just as many negative thoughts. You know they are negative because of the mix of good, bad, and gossip in their language. If they constantly pick on you, complain, and gripe about the state of the world, you need to warn them that you are on a mind diet and are taking in only what is good for you. Then, if those people remain negative, stop hanging out with them.

Frenemies, town criers, and Chicken Littles are

all poison to your outlook, so trim them from your social circle, your work, and your time online. You have this power. You may not be in a position to trim *all* contact with negative coworkers, but often you *can* choose whom you sit next to, pay attention to, and invite into your conversations. In extreme cases, you may need to "break up" with a friend or loved one. You may need to change churches or civic groups. You may even need to consider quitting your job.

Don't provide an audience for "fire starters," people who like to cause problems that only they can solve. They enjoy seeing you get upset at their nasty news, and you often reward them by thanking them for keeping you in the know.

If you spend time on Facebook, a social-networking site on which you can connect with old friends and make new ones, be judicious about the quality of your feeds (the items that appear when you log on). If people post something negative, click on the Hide button next to it. If they consistently post upsetting or negative updates, unfriend them (there's a link for this at the bottom left corner of their profile). I know this sounds harsh, but you have to ask yourself, *If my mind turns toxic, what good can I be to anyone else?*

Of course, there are some people you simply can't eliminate from your life: family members or neighbors. It may be that you have a job you are unable to leave. In those cases, learn the art of "ignoring" others. Like the kids in the classroom scenes from the *Peanuts* movies, transmute their chatter into indecipherable *wah-wah-wah* sounds. You may have done this when you were growing up and your teachers repeatedly lectured you. If so, you can do it again!

## WHAT IS THE GOOD STUFF?

I am not suggesting you stick your head in the sand, stop reading current-events coverage, and consume only inspirational or spiritual materials. The point of the good-stuff mind diet is to be highly selective about how you stay informed.

Read newspapers with an editorial style that's intended to enrich your point of view and give you necessary information that's also relevant to your life. Personally, I appreciate the *New York Times* and the *Wall Street Journal*. Both have reputations to defend, and combined they give me a snapshot of the real world. *Fast Company*, *Fortune*, *Success*, MPI's *One+*, and the *Harvard Business Review* are also great sources of constructive knowledge for me.

Listen to or watch broadcast programs that take this same approach. Although I find many radio talk shows banal,[10] most National Public Radio (NPR) content is very good: insightful, helpful, and positive in tone and intention. Oprah Winfrey and Dave Ramsey both offer helpful content as well.

Most important, read good books. If your mind diet is weighted heavily toward reading good books, you'll enlighten your perspective and gain wisdom over time. I recommend this mix in your mind diet: 25 percent media, 50 percent books, and the remaining 25 percent social and workstream (offline and online).

Books, by their nature, offer a depth of knowledge and completeness of ideas that can build you up, especially if you are reading the right ones. Good books tend to fall into four categories:

> inspirational (philosophical, psychological, or spiritual)
> instructional (personal or professional guides)
> history or reference (in both nonfiction and novel form)
> future or trends (how the world is changing)

Invest some time at your local bookstore or library perusing the stacks of books for positive mind food. If you can, invest twenty dollars a month in this plan.

Apply this to your social life too. When you look

for friends, evaluate their outlook, not just their proximity or relevance to your practical needs. When you find a conversation partner who lifts you up, commit to spending more time with him or her.

One last diet staple that will feed your mind correctly is other people's joy and happiness. Regardless of your life's path, you have the opportunity to empathetically soak up positive thoughts from others—even strangers. For example, for most people, the airport is a stressful place where harried moms and business-class bulls can easily negative you out. But if you are willing to twist your conscious mind's noticing knob, you can also discover families reuniting, kids enjoying themselves, and laughter.

Over the last year, I've been doing this to improve the emotional quality of my travel life. For example, I notice soldiers returning from the Middle East, who are frequently recognized by pilots, flight attendants, and travelers. In airport gate areas across the country, soldiers in their brown "salad suits" receive standing ovations as they walk through the terminals. I often stop, notice the recognition they are receiving, and soak up the pride they are feeling. It brings a joyful tear to my eye and loads me up with some positive energy.

During the holiday season or at birthday parties,

you also have the chance to witness others in joy mode and to celebrate with them. The same applies when someone at work receives an award.

This is what my dog likes to do: If I come home in a good mood or get excited about something, he gets in on the fun, no questions asked. He's designed that way, and he's got a great personality as a result.

## MIND FOOD FROM THE VAULT

When I was growing up, we had livestock on our farm, which gave Billye a ready source of illustrations for the various forms of mind food. "Cows eat grass and chew on their cud," she said. Her point was that there's new food and there's "regurgitation." For humans, the cud is our stored memories and the attitudes and beliefs we've formed around them. We code and store memories very quickly and then call them up later to chew on.

Much of our thinking starts with a memory, likely our number one source of mind food. It can be a memory from a moment ago (a reaction) or a memory from years ago (a reflection). We keep our memories in two vaults: our conscious mind (think of it as a computer's random-access memory [RAM]) and our subconscious (the mass storage device that serves as our ultimate backup).

The key to managing our thoughts, then, is to manage what memories we call up from the vault to redigest. Even when we manage the external mind food to a tee, in our in-between times, the vault can fill our minds with fear, resentment, and worry.

Be deliberate about calling up memory mind food, because idle thoughts allow your subconscious to run wild and dredge up random memories, many of them accompanied by negative emotions. Fear is a very powerful emotion, one almost impossible to ignore once it's been allowed to enter the psyche. This fear begs to be served, and without a plan on your part, it is fed to your mind to chew on again.

Be aware of memories entering your consciousness, and when they appear, ask yourself, *Am I bringing up a nutrient or an irritant?* Oftentimes the irritant appears noisily and has a physical manifestation, such as hot cheeks, a pit in your stomach, or a clenched fist. A nutrient can feel like a cool drink of water or a gentle high after a long run.

When you sense you are about to feed your mind a bad memory, spit it out. One way I do this is to see the negative memory as a headline on a whiteboard. Then, with my mental eraser I wipe it off the board. If it continues to try to present itself, I consciously say to myself, *Delete, please.*

We need to avoid the reintroduction of a bad memory that we've thought about before. Often we continue to generate thoughts of regret by reliving our mistakes, and we become trapped in what Billye called the "woulda shoulda coulda" trap. The more we chew on the painful past, the more details the subconscious coughs up, and the more it expands in our thinking. Once we've learned a lesson from a mistake, we need to declare the details "useless memories" and discard them. Store the insight; delete the details.

The healthiest mind food is success experiences. These are times when you displayed courage, cunning, and tenacity. You were masterful. You effortlessly performed above your own expectations. The results were positive, feedback glowed, and your confidence soared. Maxwell Maltz wrote, "We learn to function successfully by experiencing success. Memories of past success act as built-in 'stored information' which gives us self-confidence for the present task."[11]

Try this exercise the next time you are about to face a challenge. Instead of worrying, relive a relevant success experience where you excelled. Think of how courageous, creative, and/or forceful you were. Relive how well it turned out then, and consider how similar that situation is to your present task. If possible, carry a picture from the experience in your wallet or stored on your smart phone. Realize that you are the same, if not a better, person today than you were then.

A few years ago, I used this type of mind food to bolster my confidence as I prepared for a speaking engagement for the Central Intelligence Agency. Its organizers selected me to speak at a leadership event of hundreds of agents and staff and talk about the findings in my second book, *The Likeability Factor*.

During my pre-event interviews, the organizers stressed how discerning this audience could be and how often they were unimpressed by outsiders. They even shared a few stories about previous high-profile speakers who had bombed in front of this group. As much as I had prepared for the talk, I had a hard time shaking off my nervousness.

Ten minutes before I walked onstage, I relived a success experience from 2004. I vividly recalled the details surrounding my first talk for a branch of the United States military, the marines. Then, too, I was warned that the group could be difficult, especially when the speaker was a civilian. After much preparation, I gave a highly customized talk that resonated with the audience and garnered a sparkling letter of recommendation from a brigadier general.

Once I had reexperienced my talk for the marines, I visualized a copy of the recommendation letter. I could see General Catto's signature and the United States Marine Corps logo in the upper right corner. I told myself, *You rocked them then, and you'll do it again today. You are the same guy and have done just as much work to prepare for this talk as you did for that one.*

Doing this changed everything, and I relaxed and started to look forward to the talk. I confidently stepped onstage and gave the intelligence community a lively talk about personality, reading others, and making a connection. Much like my talk for the marines, it was well received, and I've been invited back again, proving that nothing succeeds like success.

Beyond success experiences, thoughts of happy times are good mind food for idle moments. Carl Erskine, a famous pitcher for the Brooklyn Dodgers, commented that bad thinking got him into more trouble than bad pitching did. He said, "One sermon has helped me overcome pressure better than the advice of any coach. . . . Its substance was that, like a squirrel hoarding chestnuts, we should store up our moments of happiness and triumph so that in a crisis we can draw upon these memories for help and inspiration."[12] Every positive emotional moment should be recognized, saved in high-definition, and stored in your conscious mind for easy access. It's easier than you think to ignore such moments or to let them get pushed out to the edges of your memory.

Now here's the upshot of feeding your mind positive memories: You push out the bad ones. As I mentioned before, your conscious mind has limited room to operate. When it gets full of the good, the bad can't find a foothold to generate thought patterns. Napoleon Hill observed, "Positive and negative emotions cannot occupy the mind at the same time."[13]

## PUTTING IT ALL TOGETHER

It's time to apply the "negative out, positive in" approach to your daily mind diet. Start in the morning with your mind's breakfast. This is the most important meal because it sets the tone for your day and instructs your subconscious about what it should notice, process, and store.

After your waking-moment exercise (we'll talk more about this in chapter 6), get out of bed slowly, giving your mind time to acclimate. If you usually spring out of bed, rush to get to work on time, and can't imagine how you'll be able to have a good mind breakfast, then get up earlier. To give your mind a chance to relax and ease into the day, you need to move s-l-o-w-l-y when you wake up.

Do not go online for the first hour you are awake.

Do not check your e-mail. That can wait. I live in California, three hours behind the East Coast. I used to worry that if I didn't read my e-mail or the day's developments first thing, I'd miss out. But I didn't. Over the last five years, I haven't missed a single opportunity because I waited one hour to subject myself to the randomness of e-mail and Internet news. Don't read the newspaper until lunch; it, too, can wait. You'll never appear dumb at work because you haven't read the latest earnings announcement, obituary column, or sports section.

Instead, do your early-morning reading in books or other high-quality publications. Study them, then purposefully think about what they mean. Make notes on what you learn. As a rule, I usually spend half the time reading spiritual and inspirational material and half reading instructional material. Between those two reads, I start my day with a positive mind-set.

At the end of your lunch hour, snatch five minutes of positive thought time to review what is going right and what positive things you'll accomplish before the day's end. Take a midafternoon break (go outside if it's a nice day). Dale Carnegie used to walk a few blocks to a church to meditate for ten minutes every afternoon, especially when his workday was stressful.

When you meditate, don't try to solve a problem; just let your mind clear.

Let your gym or commute time be good-book reading/listening time. Don't graze on whatever media those venues provide. When you get home from work, don't automatically switch on the TV. A few minutes of network television can undo a day's mind food management efforts. Before bed, read a little more, but don't try to consume complicated or overly pro-vocative content.

I've started with this principle because your mind is the key to how you think and how confident you will be. Try this daily plan, and you'll soon begin to see your thought patterns become largely optimistic, hopeful, and constructive.

**5**

# MOVE THE CONVERSATION FORWARD

Much of our lives is spent in conversations with others. When these conversations move forward, we make progress. When they go sideways, confusion reigns. When they slide backward, conflict and negative emotions ensue.

"Conversation is a game of circles," wrote Ralph Waldo Emerson.[1] In other words, a conversation is useful but often is complicated by each player's agenda. And yet, through this highly interactive process, we shape our attitudes and beliefs.

Most of your conversations take place internally, between your conscious mind and your subconscious mind. Admit it—you talk to yourself. Sometimes it's a purely mental back-and-forth, and at other times, you speak the dialogue out loud. But either way, you likely converse with yourself more often than you do with other people.

Most internal conversation involves the act of digesting mind food: *What does this information or stimulus mean? How should I feel about it? What should I do about it? Should I worry? Should I believe?* The internal conversation stands as the midpoint between your thoughts and your actions. No matter how much good stuff you put in your mind, if the internal conversation is distorted, you'll still produce negative thoughts.

Unlike real food, you have a choice when it comes to how you'll digest your mind food. You have complete control over the internal conversation. And as you'll soon see, you can apply your healthy perspective to any conversation and make it constructive each and every time.

## DUMP THE SHELLS

Billye was a master at what she called "the nut and shell exercise." When I was twelve, I went to summer church camp for the first time. It was called Singing Hills and was located just outside Albuquerque. I auditioned for a slot to sing at one of the services and was selected to perform a song on closing day. After giving a little homily on personal fulfillment, I performed "Fill My Cup," which tested the high end of my soprano register. I received a lot of compliments from other campers, but from my own church group the feedback was mixed.

Some made fun of my homemade leisure suit and my ultrahigh singing voice. One person called me "The Squealer." Gil Johnson, our adult sponsor, scolded me, saying I should have skipped the lengthy introduction and just sung the song. I took all the criticism pretty hard, and when I got home, I told Billye I would never sing again except at home.

"Criticisms are like pecans," she said, producing a handful of nuts from the pantry. "You can't swallow a pecan whole, can you? You'd never be able to properly digest it. That's what a nutcracker is for. Crack open the pecan; then you can get at the edible portion." She passed me a nut to eat.

"What should I do with the shell pieces?" she asked.

"Throw them away," I said.

"*Exactly*," she said. "Eat the nut, and dump the shells. Simple approach; works every time. Okay, think of all the things people said about your singing as a bag of pecans. Each one of those comments has something valuable inside; it makes a statement about your performance or about the person who made the comment."

"I don't get it," I said. "They made fun of me, and Mr. Johnson chewed me out for talking about the song before I sang it. They weren't giving me anything valuable."

"Yes, they were," Billye said. "Some of the kids were letting you know that they were jealous of you. Remember, 'no one ever kicked a dead dog'![2] What they said had to do with them, not you. You and I both know you can sing really well."

"What about Mr. Johnson?" I asked. "He isn't jealous."

"Gil Johnson did you a favor, because he's right; you should have just sung your song. You weren't asked to give a sermon!"

At that point, I realized something important: How you choose to digest information determines its nutritional value. And I knew that Billye was teaching me from personal experience. Years before, this had been a liberating discovery for her because she had to deal with quite a bit of information in her life, much of it potentially devastating.

When her husband left her, their two teenage sons moved away with him, which absolutely crushed

Billye. At first, she couldn't understand why they would choose him over her. Later, she found out that their decision to leave was the result of an episode in which she had disciplined them with a sweeper cord. A few weeks later, the boys had a choice between their two parents, and based on their recent experience, they chose to go with their father.

When Billye found out about this, she, too, had a choice: to learn from it or let it eat her up for the rest of her life. She was under tremendous emotional strain at the time, having to deal with a cheating husband and a bout of depression. She could have chosen to digest the information as a victim, justify her behavior toward her sons, and harden her heart.

Instead, she decided she would never whip a child again—including me. She also decided never to externalize her anger on anyone. She looked at this as a learning experience regarding punishment and emotional restraint. Once she had come to that conclusion, she swallowed the nut and dumped the shells, essentially erasing everything but the lesson from her mind.

Eventually, both sons moved back home. Their relationships with Billye were restored and to this day continue to move forward. Billye, Jim, and Mike love each other, spend time together often, and never dredge up that issue. It's been thrown out. This is a valuable lesson for you, too: You can always find a good bite in any information, even intense criticism. It says something about its author or about you— every time.

The "nut and shell exercise" is also a great way to deal with failure. Learn a lesson from what happened, and then purposefully forget the details. Maxwell Maltz often counseled his patients to actively delete everything but a failure's lesson. Later, when your subconscious considers the experience, it remembers the lesson, not the mistakes or opinions of others. The result will be a greater sense of confidence instead of worry or self-doubt.

## FRAME THE NEWS

Every day dozens of news items make their way into your mind. Some of them come from friends and colleagues, others via the media. On the face of it, few of them have a defined meaning; you give them meaning through your thoughts. To quote a line from Shakespeare's *Hamlet*, "There is nothing either good or bad but thinking makes it so."[3]

Your mind is quick to respond to all the news it pays attention to, and by default it usually positions it as either good or bad. There's rarely any in-between.

The mind tells the subconscious how you should feel about it, and the release of a host of chemicals and other physical actions are set in motion.

Your brain has a center of logical function (the neocortex) and one of emotional function (the amygdala). According to Dr. Daniel Goleman in *Emotional Intelligence*, the function of your emotional center is more powerful than the function of your logical center.[4] This means that it's really easy for incoming information to be hijacked, often coded as a 911 emergency that needs to get the juices flowing!

Most of the media and many of your acquaintances have a habit of making everything extreme, either fantastic or tragic. They love to get a response from you and have no reason to temper what they tell you. This is why you have up and down days when you feel as if your emotions are beyond your control.

This is where you need to apply your perspective, the ultimate framer of all incoming news feeds. You need to slow down your *emotional* function long enough to give your *logical* function the chance to act, somewhat like *Star Trek*'s Vulcan character Spock. If you want to take control of your emotional life, you need to accurately frame the news as it arrives in your mind. There are four ways to frame incoming information:

> *Good*—either for you or for someone or something you have an interest in
> *Neutral*—no direct effect on you or one of your interests
> *Get Busy*—adversity you need to respond to
> *Bad*—an irrevocably negative effect on you or one of your interests

Much of what you call bad news is actually get-busy news, information that gives you a reason to spring into action and focus on solutions. Get-busy news, such as a misunderstanding or a development that complicates a situation, is disturbing. Too often, you see these kinds of items, such as a loss or a defeat, and immediately frame them as negative.

In my own experience, very little news is truly bad (meaning the damage is permanent and there's nothing I can do about it). It's news that simply means, "You need to get busy and do something about this. The status quo will no longer work." Once I realized that the "bad news"

**Much of what you call bad news is actually get-busy news, information that gives you a reason to spring into action and focus on solutions.**

required me to put on my solutions hat instead of my freak-out cap, my internal conversation changed from panic to planning.

When I frame something as good news, I celebrate and tell my subconscious to park this information close to the front door so I can access it quickly. If I frame something as neutral, I throw it away, like a handful of pecan shells. If I frame it as bad and I cannot do anything about it, I recognize the emotion that goes with it and then tell my subconscious to deep-file it or delete it altogether.

## FACE THE WORST CASE

What do you do when you aren't sure whether the news is fatally bad or just highly painful? Your imagination conjured up vague images of suffering in your future, and your subconscious responds with a pit in your stomach and a breakout of sweat. Triggered by a worsening situation, your fear of the unknown is pressing on you.

Many positive thinkers might tell you to ignore bad news, not think about it, and just assume the best. But the worst-case scenario tends to grow in its enormity when you haven't faced it. In *How to Stop Worrying and Start Living*, Dale Carnegie shares a foolproof technique that Willis H. Carrier (founder of air-conditioning giant Carrier) used to conquer worrying thoughts.

Early in Willis Carrier's career, he was put in charge of installing a device at a factory that his employer owned. After Carrier had spent twenty thousand dollars on the installation, the device failed. Initially, he was petrified with worry, but after a few days he realized that worry wouldn't get him anywhere.

The first thing he did was to clearly define the worst-case scenario: He'd lose his job. The second thing he did was to accept that idea and declare that life would go on—there would be other job opportunities. The final thing he did was resolve to do better than the worst-case scenario.

With a sense of calm, he fessed up to his boss about the situation and asked for additional funds to fix the botched installation. In the end, he kept his job, and the device was soon in working order. He beat the worst, and from that day forward, he dealt with all his worries the same way.

The next time you are filled with worry, try Carrier's strategy:

1. *Define the worst case.* Ask yourself honestly, *What's the worst thing that can happen?* Once

you do that, you'll find that your imagination is getting the best of you. The reality is usually not that bad, once you clearly define it. It has the most power when it remains a mystery.

2. *Accept it as survivable.* Act as if the situation were a foregone conclusion, and let it go as a lesson to be learned. At the very least, admit that there will be some negative repercussions, regardless of your best efforts.

3. *Make a goal out of beating the worst-case scenario.* Develop a set of responses that can help you trim your losses and mitigate damages.[5]

I gave this advice to a mortgage broker from Houston whom I met while doing a taping for a cable news show in late 2008. She was talking about how the recent drop in home values had wrecked her business and her life. She felt humiliated and embarrassed by the position she was in. At this point, though, she was still speculating about her uncertain future.

"What's the worst that can happen to you?" I asked.

"I'll lose my home and have to declare bankruptcy," she replied.

"Then say good-bye to your house, and prepare yourself for a new start," I said.

"What then?" she asked.

"Well, with that pity party behind you, it's time for you to make a plan to do better than losing your house or going bankrupt. What are your options right now?"

"I can contact my bank and try to restructure my loan. I can look for a new job that leverages my direct-marketing skills. I can cut back on my expenses and turn in my lease car."

"Now you are planning for a less-than-worst-case outcome," I said.

One year later she wrote me with an update: "I lost the house, but found a great apartment. I didn't have to declare bankruptcy because I found a new job quickly and managed my other debts down. I can't believe I was so afraid. Once I said good-bye to the house and got busy working on my debt, I felt a calm release, knowing that I'd do better than my worst fears."

## END THE CONVERSATION

You've rehashed the issue and decided what you are going to do about it, but you still return to the internal conversation to chew on it some more. Unlike your external conversation partners, you are always with you—which means that the conversation can continue 24-7-365. Every time you have a free moment, the same old internal conversation can raise its head. At some point, you have to end the internal conversation about an issue or a piece of information.

If you mentally chew on something too long, it will get stuck in your psyche. Talk about something too long, and it becomes a source of irritation. Analyze something too deeply, and you'll lose touch with reality. This is why you need to cut off a conversation when it has served its logical purpose.

One time-tested piece of personal-productivity advice is never to touch a piece of paper on your desk more than twice. You touch it when it comes in to identify its nature. Then you touch it one more time to deal with it or file it away. Keep the paperwork around too long, and you end up with a cluttered desk and the nagging feeling that you can't keep up with your work!

The same goes with your internal chatter. When a get-busy piece of information shows up, face the worst and then make your plan. If you must, reflect on it once more to check your facts and affirm your plan. Then let it go. Tell yourself, "The conversation's closed, and I've moved on to a new one."

It's important that once you've made a decision, you don't give it another thought. The word *decision* stems from the Latin word *decidere*, which means "to cut off." Making a real decision "cuts off" all other options or alternatives. Once you've made your decision, there's nothing left to do but execute. It's much easier to continue the "what should I do?" debate than it is to dive into the details and get busy with what you've already committed to doing. But doing so also wastes energy. In *Psycho-Cybernetics*, Maxwell Maltz admonishes us to "do your worrying when you place your bet—not when the wheel is spinning."[6]

If you've made a mistake and made plans for being accountable for it, move on. Throw out the shells, and don't give them another thought. Billye often told me, "It's okay to make mistakes; just make new ones!" Her point was that we should not freeze ourselves in past errors. We must move forward.

## THE EXTERNAL CONVERSATION

When I was eight years old, one of my household chores was dusting. After Billye vacuumed, I'd follow behind her with an old T-shirt and use it to wipe off all the furniture. One of the hardest parts of my job was dusting the horn of plenty, which sat on our dining room table.

It was spray painted a tacky green and overflowed with artificial fruit. It was also a dust magnet. One day, as I was attempting to clean the bulbous grapes, I asked Billye, "Why do we keep this? It's old and sticky. Can't we get something that's better than this?"

"It's not just a decoration," she replied. "It's a declaration of abundance. When I was much younger, there was a terrible depression in this country. Those were times when everybody talked like sad sacks and counted the days until they lost everything. Spend time with them, and soon you'd catch the fear too. Even though Dad's farms were producing crops and our gas station was busy, he caught a case of it. The talk at the dinner table was always about the economy and who was going broke.

"One day, my mother, your granny Hattie, came home from the five-and-dime with this horn of plenty. It represented prosperity, something all of us needed to think about. She placed it in the middle of the table and waited for somebody to ask about it."

"Who said something?" I asked.

"It sat there for three nights, and finally my dad asked about it—wanted to know why she wasn't putting fresh flowers on the table instead."

"That's what I was thinking," I said.

"Your granny Hattie gave a speech that night that changed our family forever. She said that the talk around the table was holding us back and keeping our noses to the grindstone. She pointed out how much land we owned and how healthy we were. Then she stood up and announced that as of that moment, for our family, the depression was over. She made the decision that we needed to move the conversation forward and get on with our lives."

"Was the depression really over?"

"For us, yes, it was, because from that day forward, we never talked about misery or lack at the dinner table again," she said. "Instead, we started every meal with a discussion of the day's progress. For the rest of the 1930s we found opportunity right and left.

"The recovery started with this horn of plenty," Billye said. "The Great Depression didn't end one day in 1942 because the president announced it on the radio. It ended family by family as moms like mine put these baskets in the middle of the table—and declared it so."

After that, I saw the horn of plenty for what it was: a conversation piece for good, a leadership lesson about the power of our words and the impact they have on our lives. You may have seen one too, likely on your grandmother or great-grandmother's table.

Now you know why.

The words and phrases you use fuel conversations to move forward, sideways, or backward. If you inject negativity into your conversations with others, you'll generate negative thinking in yourself and in your partners.

In *Unstoppable Confidence*, Kent Sayre, a neuro-linguistic programming expert, writes, "Not only does language reflect a person's thinking, but it also reinforces a person's thinking."[7] This is true initially because you love the sound of your own voice and pay rapt attention to it. Remember, also, that your subconscious mind is an eavesdropper on every conversation you have with others. It takes careful notes and, based on your verbal instructions, produces feelings and physiological responses.

When you say that things are going from bad to worse, you are undermining your own sense of confidence. You are unwittingly instructing yourself to have a negative point of view about the present and the future.

Your words also have an impact on your conversation partners. You influence the tone and the mood and ultimately shape reality. Constant negative chatter from you can drain the energy and vitality out of others.

In 2002, while visiting a client, I witnessed this firsthand. A CEO at a software company was complaining that his team lacked backbone. Team members were quick to admit defeat and offered up excuses for every setback. The culture of his company was deteriorating, and he reckoned that the dot-com crash was the culprit.

Later that day I observed his demeanor as he addressed his employees in a weekly meeting. He focused on the bad news, the obstacles, and the weaknesses of the company and its employees. He offered no reason for anyone to believe that the company would succeed. He took no personal responsibility for the problem and instead blamed the industry as a whole and implied that his audience was part of the problem. He didn't smile once.

Standing in the back of the room, I whispered to one of his VPs, "He sounds like he's in a bad mood today."

"He's been giving this same talk for over a year," the VP replied.

At that point I realized why employee morale was low. To quote leadership author John Maxwell, when a company culture is spoiled, "that fish stinks from the head!"[8] That CEO's talk threw him into a doom loop in which his negative words created a depressed mood state, which undermined his confidence in his team and made him even more negative over time.

Even if you don't bring people down, your negative

talk will certainly drive them away. No one looks forward to conversing with a Debby Downer. Eventually, people will avoid you or, even worse, reflect negativity back to you with stinging criticism. This will drive down your own self-confidence because the negative feedback from others will make you feel as if there's something wrong with you.

On the other hand, if you are a positive partner in conversation, you'll find your team more upbeat and your own frame of mind more cheerful. You may not be able to talk your way out of a crisis by waxing on the bright side, but you can direct the dialogue toward solutions, which always adds a dose of confidence to the mix.

The key to positive conversations is to project your confident outlook by selecting the right words, saying them in the proper tone of voice, and assuming a constructive role. Get all three of these talking components right, and you'll generate enthusiasm and courage in others (and in yourself), as you'll see in the remainder of this chapter.

## TRIM YOUR VOCABULARY

First things first: You need to eliminate "weak" words and phrases from your personal vocabulary. Take the word *lucky*. When you say someone was lucky when he or she achieved success, you are making an excuse for that person's achievement. The use of that word tends to mystify success and consequently to make it impossible for others to achieve purposefully.

### Lose Lucky-Lacky Language

In *The Magic of Thinking Big*, David Schwartz confronts this way of talking when he writes, "Conquer Luck Excusitis. . . . Accept the law of cause and effect. Take a second look at what appears to be someone's 'good luck.'"[9] Physical laws, not luck, determine the bounce of the ball. "The that's-the-way-the-ball-bounces approach teaches us nothing."[10]

In my travels, the name of Mark Cuban, the founder of Broadcast.com, comes up often. I got my big break in business when I went to work for him in 1998. He sold his company to Yahoo! at the height of the dot-com bubble, took a billion dollars off the table, and now owns a few other companies, including the NBA's Dallas Mavericks. "Wow, Mark sure was lucky!" is a comment I've heard dozens of times, but I've never heard it come out of the mouth of a true entrepreneur.

The truth is, Mark wasn't lucky; he was smart and decisive. He aggressively built up the company's assets, negotiated powerfully with Yahoo!, and then had the foresight to sell the stock at the right time. Sure, he had a little help from the stock market and a few advisers and partners. But calling him lucky disrespects the law of cause and effect. He was aiming for his success the entire time.

Closely related to the word *lucky* are "lacky-isms" such as *shortfall, lack, worry/worried, I fear,* or *if only I could.* All these words or phrases signal a sense of defeat, typical speak for an anxious "follower." Talk long enough about what you lack, and soon the only people who will hang out with you are "lackys." Dr. Peale urged his readers to specifically eliminate fretting from their discussions when he wrote, "Snip off the little worries and expressions of worry" like little branches atop a tall tree.[11] If you are truly worried, sharing your concerns with others is like sharing a cold to help yourself feel better. You don't feel better; you just make someone else feel worse.

Stop using tentative words; they hedge conversations to the point of being meaningless. The unconfident person talks with qualifiers and commits to very little. Tentative words include *maybe, perhaps, might, somehow, allegedly, no offense, just saying, should, unlikely, probably, possibly, likely, may, could be, appears, suggests, leads one to think,* and so on.

If you want to project confidence, say what you

believe, and say it directly. You'll find that once the namby-pamby words are gone, confident statements remain. One way you can examine your vocabulary is to audit the e-mails you've sent on a challenging or stressful day. Were you using power words or lucky-lacky ones? It's a good idea to audit your e-mails periodically to measure your improvement. Sam Knoll, a Novell employee who took one of my e-mail training courses, did this, and in less than ninety days he saw a dramatic change in his vocabulary—and an added benefit: "When I reviewed three days of my own e-mails, I was floored by how wimpy I wrote. I printed several of them out and circled the weak words and luck-lack language. In just a few reading sessions, I realized that I needed to proof my notes differently in the future—for strength as well as grammar. Now my e-mails are crisp and authoritative. They are also much shorter!"[12]

Another category of weak language is the time-machine variety. When you evoke "back in the day," you are waxing nostalgic, which is not a useful way to think of the past. Today is the day, and to the confident, tomorrow will be even better.

When you talk about success coming to you "someday" (e.g., "Someday, I'll be recognized and promoted"), you might as well say "with a little luck."

The word *someday* makes a mystery out of the future. If you want to talk about success in the future, talk cause and effect: "When I crush my numbers at work, I will be promoted." That's the confident way to talk!

## RING A POSITIVE TONE

In every conversation, you have a choice: Will it have a positive or a negative tone? You exercise that choice in your salutation or your response. For example, when someone asks you, "How are you?" or "How is it going?" your response will likely dictate the course of the conversation from that point on unless your conversation partner isn't listening.

More than you would think, though, the other person *is* listening. When you say, "I'm getting by," or "Okay, I guess," you are establishing your lack of confidence. This is even more likely when circumstances are truly challenging. By calling attention to the state of the economy, your own fears, or negative developments, you shift the subject of the conversation from progress to obstacles.

Complaining about your health to anyone who is not your doctor is also a way to drive a conversation toward the negative. You will never feel better because you complain about your back. In fact, you'll likely feel worse as you instruct your subconscious to focus on your aches and pains.

One way to drive a conversation toward the positive is to answer the perfunctory "How's it going?" with an honest but positive answer—the more specific the better. Recently when someone asked me how I was doing, I said, "Great! I'm working on my book today, and I'm filled with ideas for the chapter I'm writing." This signals momentum and shifts the conversation to project a tone of progress.

When you kick off a conversation, ask a question that begs for a positive answer, such as "What's the good word?" This is the advice Dale Carnegie gave his adult-education students. He admonished them to drive the discussion away from hard times and toward progress. Author and marketing consultant Keith Ferrazzi opens conversations with "What are you working on these days?" Often his conversations end up focusing on his partners' opportunities, exciting projects, and personal interests.

When conversations start out with problems, direct them toward solutions. To bellyache about the problem is to expand it in both the other person's mind and yours. To assign blame or fault for the problem freezes the conversation in the past.

When I served as chief solutions officer at Yahoo!,

I was frequently dispatched to respond to critical situations such as the loss of a major customer or the need to deal with a million-dollar misunderstanding with a partner. We had a group of young employees, many of them lacking in real-world crisis-management experience. I could see it in their faces. When they told me what the problem was, I never responded by ticking off a list of what we lacked or were up against. Instead, I began the conversation by saying, "First, let's itemize what we have to work with. What resources can we bring to bear on this situation?" Instead of communicating "First, we *lack*," I proclaimed, "First, we *have*." In short order, worry was converted to excitement as the conversation became solutions-centered.

Whenever possible, inject positive or decisive words into a conversation. One of the most positive words you can use is *yes*. Use it as often as you can. It evokes agreement and support. *Certainly*, *absolutely*, *exactly*, *definitely*, and *sure* denote confidence or support as well. When you speak about others, use encouraging words, but be authentic. "Good for him!" is a positive way to respond when you hear about another person's success.

A Peale-like way to move a conversation forward is to inject declarations of your confidence in other people. Stand up for your teammates by stating your belief that they will be successful. It will encourage your conversation partners and reinforce your feeling of total confidence. Never criticize people who are not present to defend or explain themselves. And never predict that another person will experience failure.

Beyond words, let your inflection and body language support your positive vibe. Smile, nod encouragingly, and display openness. My dog sets a positive tone when we interact. He shakes his tail approvingly, and it works every time! Don't let your sentences drop off like rocks falling down a cliff. Let your words be like a prayer, always rising upward.

You may have a social-media outlet such as Facebook or Twitter or a blog. Make your updates positive in both content and tone. Declare, "Today we are rich!" I'm sure if Billye were a Facebooker, "Today we are rich!" would be her eternal update. Don't be the town crier, always posting links to disturbing political or news developments. Use your Internet social influence to "accentuate the positive," in the words of songwriter Johnny Mercer.

## BE A COLLABORATOR

The role you assume in a conversation can determine its direction. Be a builder of ideas, not a destroyer of dreams. Be a partner, not a detractor. Be a collaborator whenever possible.

What's the opposite of the collaborator-builder-partner? The devil's advocate, and they are worth a dime a dozen. Many times in your life, people will likely respond to one of your ideas by saying, "Now, let me play devil's advocate with you." They have no idea what they are talking about.

The concept of the devil's advocate was created in the sixteenth century to ensure the quality of candidates considered for canonization, or sainthood. A church official would assign the role to a lawyer, and the lawyer would be charged with building a case *against* the candidate, one based largely on the candidate's character. Usually the candidate was one of the most revered men or women in the community and was considered above reproach. The devil's advocate's job was to snoop around in an attempt to dig up dirt and eventually to testify against the saintly person. That's why it's called devil's advocate. Most lawyers were asked to take this role only once during their careers. It was not a position for which any smart person would volunteer!

Today, it's assumed that the devil's advocate is a useful conversation partner. If that assumption has been a part of your talking tool kit for years, let me convince you to lose it ASAP. When you interrupt someone at the first opportunity to gracefully take on the role of devil's advocate, you are starting a debate, not a conversation. You launch objections with a tone of voice that suggests, "Have you even considered the obvious?" when in fact the other person has likely considered that objection from the beginning.

Although you may think you are preventing a disaster, research suggests that devil's advocates actually bolster people's beliefs that they are right and that you are against *them* (not the idea). You should reply with your objection only when you truly disagree with the *premise* of the idea, not merely with its finer points. If you interrupt the conversation with your barrage of reality checks, you'll likely fluster others and bring out negative emotions. This will reinforce your doubt in them and leave you to wonder, *Am I the only smart person here?*

I've never met devil's advocates with many good ideas. Usually they are compensating for their lack of creativity by being nitpicky. Their negativity isolates them over time, as idea people eventually shun them. They end up with a point of view that's anti-change, anti-risk, anti-new. Mostly I see "Can I play devil's advocate for a minute?" as a form of asking permission to put someone on the defensive—a psychological form of bullying.

The next time someone is casually telling you about an idea she has, let her finish describing it completely. You might be concerned that without the devil's advocate, we'll have a lot of mistakes in the world, but there's an alternative. At the end of the presentation, ask her to name a few obstacles the plan would need to get over. Almost every time, you'll hear the same ones that came to you as you heard the idea. The tone, however, will be positive as the speaker lays out the objection and her answer to it because she's driving the conversation.

In both improvisational comedy and business innovation, there is a collaboration device called the "yes-and" routine. When one person suggests something, you build on it by saying, "Yes, and then we should do this," or, "Yes, and then we could take it that way." I watched comics Louie Anderson and Kyle Cease do this one day over lunch at one of their Stand-Up Boot Camp clinics where I spoke. They took a simple joke and expanded it into an entire skit. "Taking the yes-and approach leaves the line open for creative ideas," Louie told me later. "The first time someone jumps in with a 'but-what-about' question, the line of thinking is cut off."

At some point, your creative partner will need to make a pitch to the bank or the boss, whose role is to shoot down ideas in order to minimize risk. Let that person be the "bad guy." You be the builder of ideas, the explorer of concepts, and the promoter of innovation. You'll find that you will generate excitement both internally and externally and lead others to see you as a great person off whom to bounce ideas.

## CONFRONT THE CHICKEN LITTLES

One negative-minded person can undermine the culture of an entire group. This is especially true during times of struggle, when paranoia is seen as a form of prudence. I call those people who have pessimistic viewpoints or an expressed sense of impending doom Chicken Littles ("The sky is falling! The sky is falling!").

No matter how well you handle your side of the conversation, at some point you need to step up and lead the conversation forward. You cannot wait for the Chicken Littles to follow your example, as they can harness the emotions of fear and anger in others faster than you can inspire or give hope.

In 2001, Greg Coleman left *Reader's Digest* to run North American operations at Yahoo!. Over three decades he had survived multiple recessions and dozens of rounds of changes in his market. When he came to Yahoo!, he immediately noticed that most managers were freaked out by the economy and, by 2003, by a competitor named Google.

"It's like an Outward Bound project here sometimes," he once told me. "Everyone is acting as if we are in a struggle for survival. We are not! We've got to flip this conversation around into a positive one. Chicken Little must fry!"

Every day Greg received more than one hundred internal e-mails, many of them from paranoid employees who "thought he'd like to hear this bad piece of news." He'd single out repeat offenders, print out the notes, write the words *Chicken Little* across the top with a marker—then return them via interoffice mail. It didn't take long to get the message across!

One of Greg's managers was so inspired by this act of leadership that he had a self-inking "Chicken Little" stamp made so he could stamp all the negative notes he received and then post them in the commons on the "wall of shame."

After I shared this story at the Willow Creek Association's Leadership Summit in 2004, a small-business owner took it to heart and had his own stamp made. In less than a year he reported a change in the mood at work: "Reward behavior and you get more of it. Up until I heard you speak, I treated the bad news brigade like they were adding value—like a junkyard owner treats his pit bull for barking at strangers. Now I reward the people who bring in the good word, and our company culture is stronger than ever. People are happy to work here, and we are staying focused on the solution, not the problem."

Napoleon Bonaparte once said, "The leader's role is to describe reality, and give hope."[13] If you want to lead others, push the conversation toward balance, not toward lopsidedness in fear and worry. "Reality" is frequently defined by the powers that be, and then its negative elements become amplified throughout an organization. This is why adversity can trigger panic in the troops. There are too many Chicken Littles and not enough da Vincis. When you confront the naysayers and doomsdayers, you are leading the conversation forward.

◼

To get his own company out of the doom-and-gloom rut, my friend Eric moved the conversation forward by creating a reading club with his top sales reps. They discussed the books they were reading and what they were learning and then applied that knowledge to their own situations. It was a simple effort that produced unexpected results.

"Taking a page from one of our reading club's

picks, *Good to Great*, we established a core value for our sales region that we could focus on and be excited about: People are our priority!" Eric told me during one of our "counseling sessions."

"Your people?" I asked.

"All people in our path," he answered. "Customers, partners, anyone we met with. We committed to making a positive difference in their lives using office leasing as a platform to spend time together."

"Excellent approach," I said. "Giving to be rich."

"Exactly," he replied. "Got our minds off the news and into the world of people solutions. We helped out-of-work entrepreneurs find money and jobs. We helped partners find new customers."

"How's your business doing?" I asked, shifting the focus from giving to gaining.

"That's the great thing," he said. "We have gone from red to black in two quarters, mostly due to referrals and a real prospecting intensity on the part of my team. We have a whiteboard at the office that tracks the 'manna' falling into our region every week."

"So the mood at work is improved?" I asked. (After all, 2002 was not a great year, as the recession continued and many lost hope that things would ever get back to normal in the tech world.)

"We are on fire!" he said, with the zeal of the "rock

star" Eric I knew from days past. "We believe in something bigger, something far more powerful than making money. We are focused on helping others, which makes us oblivious to ourselves. You can imagine how different that makes us in the market!"

"So, you're out-hustling the competition?"

"It's more than effort," he replied. "By focusing on creating opportunities for others, we've earned more business in the last six months than countless cold calls could have yielded. We're also leasing at higher profits. Our clients want us to succeed."

That's moving the conversation forward in action. It's not just about the conversation; it's really about changing the future for the better.

# 6

# EXERCISE YOUR GRATITUDE MUSCLE

A few years ago over dinner, my son, Anthony, expressed his intention to leave his current job to explore greener pastures. He was working as a "Genius" (a computer-repair professional) at one of Apple's flagship stores in Los Angeles. It was his first postcollege job, and he had worked really hard to land it, beating out hundreds of other applicants in the process.

"I'm thinking of leaving the company," he announced, between bites. "They don't appreciate me like they used to. Shift schedules aren't drawn up until the last minute, and recently, they've been making me work weekends. I can do better."

Stunned, I dropped my fork. We'd been bragging to our friends for months about the wonderful opportunity Anthony had at Apple. He had some stock equity, health-care benefits, and a salary that I could only have dreamed of in my twenties. For a design-freak techie like Anthony, Apple is arguably one of the best places in the world to work.

"And the atmosphere," he continued. "It's getting negative. Apple has strict rules for repairs and returns, and that leaves me on the receiving end of some pretty intense complaints from our customers. I'm not looking forward to going in every day like I used to."

"What will you do?" I asked.

"Anything I want," he replied. "I can land a job at any other computer-service company or retailer out there. They'd all want me for my Apple experience. We've got the heat."

My first inclination was to launch into a lecture about how incredible Apple is. At that time, fall 2008, the most exciting place in the mall was the Apple store. The company's success with the iPhone dominated the headlines everywhere.

But just as I was about to open my mouth, I caught myself, realizing that no words I could say would change Anthony's point of view. I also remembered an old saying from my Yahoo! days: "Feelings are facts." They are not opinions offered up for my judgment or correction. To change my son's perspective, I needed to create an experience for him that would change the way he felt about working at Apple.

We had already planned to spend the next day running some errands related to his car's upcoming inspection and registration. I used our time together as an opportunity to stage a Dickensian "jobs of the past, present, and future" experience for Anthony.

Driving down Sunset Boulevard in east Hollywood, I pointed out the home-improvement center where he'd worked when he was in high school.

"You could get your old job back there," I said. "I bet they'd love to have you. You're as able-bodied as ever."

"Yuk," he replied.

We could see a few employees with weight belts on, loading huge bags of cement mix into a contractor's truck. They were sweating profusely.

"They call those guys lifers," Anthony said. "They'll do that their whole lives to have a steady check and health-care bennies. It's backbreaking work. For that matter, I don't ever want to work with my hands again."

I remember smiling to myself and thinking, *One down, two to go.*

After lunch we stopped by an office-supply store to pick up some envelopes and blank media. It was a cavernous place, empty of customers and dead silent. The employees stared blankly into space, some of them passing the time by fiddling around on their wireless phones.

"What about this place?" I asked him. "I'll bet they'd bend over backward to get a guy with your experience in their computer department. You could probably negotiate working only weekdays here."

"Are you kidding?" he replied. "This place is a morgue. Dead. Besides, it's going nowhere. Places like this will be closed in a few years. Because of iPhones and computers, we don't need paper, file folders, paper clips, or pens anymore. This place is so '80s."

"All stores are dead at times," I countered. "You said you wanted to work at a place that appreciates you, and I bet you would be cherished here!"

"You don't get it," he said. "At my store, I meet musicians and movie stars, hip people, and sell them the cutting edge of technology—not legal pads and staplers!"

*Two down; he's about to come around.*

Our last stop of the day was the dreaded Department of Motor Vehicles, where we'd likely spend an hour or two in various lines as we navigated all the forms related to getting his car's registration renewed.

It was a dingy place filled with impatient customers and staffed by workers who, it seemed, couldn't have cared less about offering a positive service experience. Gum-chewing clerks dispassionately informed applicants that they were either in the wrong line or lacked necessary paperwork.

"This is a place where you could make your mark!" I proclaimed. "You could bring the Apple Genius experience to bear, and they'd probably put you in charge in less than a year. They'd shower you with awards and give you a sweet Monday-through-Friday schedule."

"Are you serious?" Anthony replied. "This is awful. I've never dealt with customers as ticked off as these people are at the DMV. And the people I would work with here—no way! They don't care about us at all, and they don't seem to care about each other, either."

He went on to explain how much camaraderie he had with his current coworkers, their shared interests and passion for solving customers' problems. They often went out to eat together after work and socialized on the weekends. During our drive back to my house, Anthony talked about working at Apple, and gratitude for his job began to ooze out.

"Maybe Apple is a great opportunity after all," he said. "I was really glad to get that job in the first place, and it's still the best company in the world. I was just a little burned-out, I guess."

By the end of our day, he was fully recommitted to Apple, and he works there happily as I write this. He's now tuned in to what's going right and how much he has to be grateful for in his job. He's had to refresh his gratitude since then, because it constantly needs attention, but now he refreshes it himself.

As Billye would say, Anthony lost his gratefulness through neglect, but through some exercise, he got it back! That was one of the home-baked confidence concepts she often referred to when my attitude about an opportunity was poor.

"Gratitude is a muscle, not a feeling," she told me one day during my junior year of high school. "If it was a feeling, you'd feel it all the time, now wouldn't you?"

Like Anthony, I had been grumbling about my job. I was a DJ at the local radio station. I had begged for that job (and the high profile it offered me). But within a few months, I had decided my late-night weekend shift was ruining my social life.

"You've got to give your gratitude muscle a work-out every day if you want to *feel* grateful," Billye continued. "People who don't spend time on this muscle get spiritually flabby over time and forget to appreciate the very things they wished for. Their souls get out of shape without proper exercise."

Over the years, I realized she was right. You can't just change your feelings, but you *can* change your daily habits to strengthen your *sense* of gratitude, which will then produce feelings of gratefulness that will reinvigorate you.

Consider the new-hire employee. He's so happy just to get the job. On the first day he floats into work, light as a feather—grateful for the opportunity. He marches around with boundless energy for his tasks, often spouting positive comments: "Can you believe it? Coffee is free!" or "I love this job! I can't believe I'm getting paid to be here."

A few years later, if he has not been exercising his gratitude muscle at work, his attitude changes for the worse. To another new hire who shows up gung ho and skippy, he snarls, "Calm down. It's not as good as you think. If you don't turn it down a notch, you're going to make the rest of us look bad."

That's what a lack of attention to your gratitude muscle can do to you. Gratitude, then, is a capability built up through exercise and focus. It's an ability to perceive, receive, and produce the positive emotion of gratefulness.

After a great experience or a windfall, you'll experience a temporary shot of gratitude, just as an energy drink gives you a jolt of stamina. But over time, it fades away.

To strengthen a muscle, be it physical, emotional, or spiritual, you need to task it and stretch it. In this case, you need to work out your gratitude muscle to produce gratefulness as your dominating thought.

Now I want to talk about a plan that will give your gratitude muscle a serious workout. This workout has three parts: tuning in, digging deeper, and expressing thanks.

## TUNE IN

The difference between a grateful person and an ungrateful person lies in perception: One sees a life of beauty; the other sees a life of lack. This explains how someone who is poverty-stricken can find joy in spite of his or her circumstances while many wealthy people can often be miserable in spite of virtually limitless resources. This also accounts for how many who are terminally ill can still find hope while many healthy people focus only on the obstacles in life.

When we have a significant reason to notice the bounty, such as a promotion at work, it's easy to let gratefulness flood our senses. But we often miss the more subtle wins in life because we don't make an effort to notice and appreciate them.

That makes sense, though, given the world we live in. Hundreds of marketing messages are aimed at us daily. We have lists of to-dos and must-reads that distort our perceptions. Our roles and obligations clamor for our attention. For most of us, the *default* approach in life is to pay attention to the "ugly" and urgent and live in survival mode.

What we need to do is instruct our subconscious, the great hard drive and processor in our heads, to notice and record the beauty in our lives. Maxwell Maltz wrote, "It is *conscious thinking* which is the 'control knob' of your unconscious machine."[1] Although we can't program our feelings directly, when we direct our subconscious to tune in to the good in life, we will deeply influence them.

When it comes to finding reasons to be grateful—I think of them as avenues of appreciation—it helps to follow a practice I call the POET approach, which stands for People, Opportunities, Experiences, and Things. I put People first because taking note of their greatness in your life feeds your confidence in others. I put Things last because they cause us to focus on material items that can either be in short supply or be taken away entirely.

How do you know when you should feel grateful? When someone or something gives you a positive thought, that's a sure sign that you should add it to your list. Behind every smile lies something to be noticed and appreciated. This also lowers your threshold on what it takes to make you grateful. Learn to recognize a "micro thrill" or a minor pleasantry as an item to be added to your list of reasons to be grateful. Here's your first assignment: Make a daily list of five "avenues of appreciation" about your personal life. Be as specific as possible; avoid generalities such as nice weather or being alive (although there's nothing wrong with being grateful for those, too). The truth is, the more specifically you pinpoint each item on your list and how it makes you feel, the better the exercise will be. Log these observations in a journal or some other place where you can easily go back to them. Leave ample space after each item on your list.

Try this with your work life too. Write a list of five things you appreciate about your role at work. Focus as much as possible on the people you interact with and how they support you or how you get to support them. Role-based gratitude is a great generator of appreciation for coworkers, as well as for your boss.

It won't come easy in the beginning because we aren't tuned in to these types of things in our daily routines. Instead, we often tune in to fires that need to be put out. If we are feeling resentful, we tune in to things to resent.

To fill out your list, give yourself a few snatches of still time to look around for reasons to be grateful. Being still allows you to pick out objects of gratitude, which are often buried in your life's information traffic jam. Preserve the last ten minutes of your lunch hour to do this, or use a break in the afternoon for this exercise.

One way to stretch your gratitude muscle is to change your daily routine. When you're shopping or driving to work, pretend you are a first-time visitor to your city. Shop at different stores, change the route or mode of transportation you use to get to work. When you jar your perceptive routine, new avenues of appreciation, previously buried in the rut of your daily routine, will emerge.

Shake things up at work, too. Remember Eric Goldhart? His business was rocked, again, by the market decline that started in 2008. To battle the collective economic funk at the office, he used new-hire gratitude as a remedy. He and his team take one morning a month to meet as "new hires" and collaborate to come up with a list of all the assets and positive developments the company has at its disposal.

After the first meeting, he saw results: "The list got me excited. I was more excited than I had been in months. As 'new hires' we were able to leave behind all the baggage from the last eighteen months. We are almost skipping down the hallway with energy, excitement, and passion for being at this company during this particular time in history."

Reexamine the things you see every day to purposefully discover positive attributes in them. When you see a building, tune in to its architecture and fine appointments. Notice the beauty it adds to your view. At lunch, look at your plate of food, and see a feast—one that would be appreciated by millions of hungry people around the world. Savor each bite. Don't stare blankly at the horizon at the end of the day; focus on the sunset's awesome calmness. Pick out its pastel colors.

Recruit a workout partner for this exercise. It could be a member of your family, a close friend, or a coworker. Make a deal: Each day, you'll help the other person notice what he or she should appreciate, and that person will do the same for you. It's a two-way street, however; you are not looking for someone who's a self-appointed "voice of reality" to preach to you, and you shouldn't be that to the other person.

Ask God to help you be a better noticer, to

recognize the fruits of life instead of the setbacks. Billye's prayers often included pleas for God to give her signs that things would get better and for the wisdom to see them and gather strength.

In the previous chapter, we talked about avoiding a time-machine variety of weak language, one that focuses on the past or an indefinite future. But when it comes to gratitude, a time-machine mentality is a positive thing. So think of a time in your past when you had far less to give thanks for. Recollect when you thought, *If only I could get out of this mess, I'd be happy!* Think of your younger days, when you said, "If only I had my own car, a home, a good job, someone who loves me . . . I'd finally be happy."

Lock in on those memories, and you'll soon realize that the someday you wished for is today. You likely have at least some of what you dreamed about then, but over time you've raised the bar and forgotten about those "bargains" you made in your youth.

Looking back from this vantage point, *Today you are rich!*

When I sit cramped in an airplane seat on a tarmac for hours, I recall those times from my twenties when I dreamed of traveling the world. I remember how much I wanted to see the sights and meet new people. Eventually the exercise overwhelms me with gratitude and allows me to forget, at least temporarily, that I'm locked in travel captivity for a few more hours. I stretch my legs and soul in one motion—and smile.

Now think about your future. Identify an opportunity in the next year that could turn out well—and possibly change your situation for the better. Imagine how the ball will bounce your way, how out of the blue, people will help you, and how you'll be successful beyond your wildest dreams. You can do it. To paraphrase Dr. Peale, "If you can worry, you can imagine success!"

Think of an upcoming vacation or a leisure activity, and focus on how much you're looking forward to it and how great it will make you feel. Think of the sights, tastes, and sounds you'll experience and the people you'll get to share that time with. This is like licking the frosting off the spoon hours before the cake will be served to company.

As you flood your mind with thoughts of a bright future, you'll find yourself looking forward to life instead of dreading it. You'll temper any inconveniences or struggles in the present moment with a promise of a better tomorrow, and you'll tune in to the possibilities of life.

## DIG DEEPER

At this point in the workout, you are tuned in and noticing the things for which you can be grateful. But the act of noticing uses just the surface layer of your gratitude muscle. As with any workout regimen, you need to get past the surface muscles to really tone up and build strength.

If you want to pump up the gratefulness, you'll need to dig deeper into your life situation. You'll need to plumb areas of your psyche that you do not usually visit, and it might feel a bit uncomfortable, a little like how a new stretch can feel on a seldom-used muscle.

Erwin McManus, a friend and fellow author, developed an exercise to jiggle the perspective of anyone feeling ungrateful. He poses this question: "What do you deserve?" In most cases the thoughtful answer is powerful: nothing.[2]

The truth is, we deserve few, if any, of the things we've come to expect, wish for, or covet in the lives of others. The answer to my friend's question recasts our point of view and helps us to understand that we should be grateful for the most basic things in life and never let our expectations define our level of thankfulness.

Another way to dig deeper is to ask yourself what average outsiders would think about your current situation. Would they feel pity, or would they envy you? What would those who are less fortunate think about your plight or opportunity? Would they think you've lost your gratefulness?

Recently I had an *aha* moment while my wife and I were visiting Barcelona, Spain. Our apartment had no air-conditioning, and the weather was hot and sticky. I couldn't sleep because of the heat, and after five days I was a moody mess. I groused and complained about the horrible accommodations. Poor me! (During those days in Barcelona, I was also touring historic churches, eating delectable tapas, and enjoying World Cup playoff matches with joyous locals. But I guess the heat made me "forgetful.")

On the last day of the trip, I was taking a shower and still muttering to myself about how I was having a terrible time and couldn't wait to get back to my own home's creature comforts. I even had the silly thought that I wished I'd never taken this trip. Then a question popped into my head: *If you posted pictures from your trip on Facebook with a narrative about the miserable heat, would your friends feel sorry for you or wish they had been in Barcelona too?* The answer hit me like cold water from the showerhead: *You are incredibly fortunate, albeit a little sweaty. Millions of people would gladly trade places with you, and many of them live in hotter conditions in much less beautiful surroundings!*

Then I heard a chiding voice from my childhood. It was Billye's, reminding me that in these situations, "You can get glad in the same pants you got mad in!"

It occurred to me that just five days earlier, newly arrived in town, I had marveled at the Gothic design of the Born district where I was staying. I had savored the ham-and-cheese baguette sandwiches the city was famous for—yet somehow I'd let it all wear off.

What had really changed? Nothing—except that I had lost my gratefulness.

I had a few hours left before we needed to head to the airport for the flight home, so I took advantage of my new perspective and went outside to take in the beauty. I noticed the design of the Santa Maria del Mar, a historic church just steps from my apartment. I smelled the wonderful aromas of the bakery at the end of the street. I recalled the art I'd seen, the friendly people I had met, and the merchants who had bent over backward to serve me.

By the time I climbed into the airport taxi, I was envious of myself! I realized how fortunate I was to have had this trip. Heat or no heat, that was the only realistic picture I could paint.

Here's another way to deepen your gratitude:

Identify the source for all the opportunities, experiences, and relationships you appreciate. Your job, the life-changing trip you took last year, your home, your car—all of these came from a source who cares about you and is thoughtful toward you. The immediate source could be a person or a group of people, but ultimately the source of all these good things is God.

In some cases, it was the encouragement of others who gave you the motivation to seize an opportunity, to develop your talent, or to go after a particular experience. No one achieves any great heights in life alone. There's always a supportive source.

**When you begin to exercise gratefulness toward a "who" and not just appreciation for the "what," you are extending gratitude fully.**

Go back to your list of "avenues of appreciation." (I hope one day you'll have dozens of those items in a journal.) In each instance, next to or underneath the item, write down the names of those who made it possible.

Consider their intentions as they gave to you, helped you, or supported you. You'll realize how much people care about you and want you to be successful and happy. When you begin to exercise gratefulness toward a "who" and not just appreciation for the "what," you are extending gratitude fully.

This will boost your confident outlook. Through gratitude you'll feel the power of your community and how it covers for your shortfalls. When you attribute all that you have to someone outside yourself, you deflect the glory and begin to celebrate the synergistic power of a team.

## START YOUR DAY WITH GRATITUDE

Now that you know how to dig deeper, you are ready for a daily exercise that will change your life: Each morning when you wake up, make gratitude your first thought. Your waking moments set the tone for your entire day by directing your subconscious to focus on some things and to ignore others.

In *The Magic of Thinking Big*, psychologist David Schwartz wrote, "A humorist once said the most difficult problem in life was getting out of a warm bed into a cold room."[3] His point is that waking up can be a shock to the system. But if you devote just five to seven minutes every morning to the following practice, you'll start getting up on the grateful side of the bed instead of muttering, "How am I going to get through this day?"

When you first wake up, run cold water over a

washcloth. For maximum effect, keep a wet washcloth in the refrigerator overnight. Wring out the excess water, and fold the cloth into a three-inch-wide strip.

Get back into bed (set a second alarm if you're afraid you'll fall back to sleep), and place the cold washcloth over your eyes. This will help keep you awake.

Lie very still. Scan your memory banks from the previous day to locate two people who helped you or somehow contributed to your life. You might have experienced a success yesterday enabled by something someone did days or weeks ago. It could be work related, family related, or something more casual. As the faces of those people float into your mind, say their names out loud (you might have to whisper if your spouse is still sleeping). Now, say the names again, but this time add a description of what each person did for you and the difference it made.

It's better if you are able to say these thoughts of gratitude out loud, because doing so cements a grateful attitude in your subconscious.

Now it's time to advance gratitude for the coming day. Think of someone you predict will assist you today. Maybe that person did something in previous days that will manifest in goodness for you today. Identify that person by name and describe what you anticipate he or she will do for you and what a difference it will make to the day's success.

It's okay if your list includes the same people from day to day. In the beginning it likely will. When I first started this exercise, my wife and a few close colleagues made the list every morning. But over time, my list has expanded as my gratefulness has attracted more "helpers" into my life, and I've become more aware of those who contribute to any success I experience.

When you finish this exercise, you'll be ready to spring out of bed with energy. You'll feel a sense of confidence that you are on a roll and that you are not alone in life. When you encounter the people on your list, your demeanor with them will change, and that often results in their doing more of what you appreciated in the first place.

I've road tested this exercise and found that in every case, it's worth the time and effort. For example, in 2010 I conducted a nonscientific study of a few dozen people who agreed to follow this exercise for at least a month. To a person, they all reported that this way of kicking off the day helped them to have a more positive outlook on life and an appreciation for all the support they had around them. One story, though, stands out as a testimony to the additional benefits that come from early-morning gratefulness.

Paula Cooper, one of the study participants, read about this exercise at a time when she needed an emotional lift. "My life has been unbelievably chaotic, so I'm really glad you offered this exercise when you did," she wrote. Then she continued:

> For the past two years, my husband has been pursuing a job in Maryland [they were living in Detroit at the time], due to information technology jobs being outsourced. When he landed one with the government in Annapolis, I knew it was the right thing for us to do. But it was hard, I grew up in Michigan and all my friends and family were here. At the same time, my father, who had been ill for five years, had surgery to remove a cancer tumor.
>
> All of this stress was causing me to wake up earlier than I wanted to, never being able to sleep past 7 a.m. I would wake up worrying. Then your exercise came along, and I started to do it instead of just lying there, thinking about what I needed to do that day. Each morning as I awoke, I closed my eyes and envisioned the two people who helped me the day before. Sometimes it was a clerk in a store, usually though, it was a coworker or a friend who was helping me with the move. After

*thinking of these people, I felt more invigorated and focused. I was ready to attack the day. I felt like I had already accomplished something before even getting out of bed!*

Then Paula surprised me with an innovation on the exercise:

*On the day of the big move, I was feeling really stressed and the day was crazy. We had too much stuff to fit into our much smaller house. The moving truck was blocking the street, upsetting our new neighbors. My cat crawled up the chimney and wouldn't come down. I was freaking out! So I decided to do my gratitude exercise right there in the middle of the day.*

*I wet a cloth with cold water and found a quiet spot in the backyard. I did the exercise in just a few quiet minutes. It calmed me down and shifted my thoughts to gratitude for all the things that were going right that day. I realized the movers were quick, efficient, and really nice guys. I realized that the cat would come down when everything settled down. At that point, I was in a cheerful mood, thanking everyone involved profusely, and got on with the day.*

What a great testimonial.

We've finished the first two aspects of our work-out—tuning in and digging deeper—and now we're ready for the third aspect, the importance of *expressing* gratitude.

## EXPRESS YOUR GRATITUDE

Gratitude not expressed is thanks not given. *Foundations of Faith* author William Arthur Ward is credited as having written, "Feeling gratitude and not express-ing it is like wrapping a present and not giving it." Your words of appreciation can reward others and inspire onlookers, so don't keep them bottled up inside you!

When you share your feelings of gratefulness, you paint yourself into a positive corner with others and, more important, with yourself. The words we speak influence our point of view deeply; they code our beliefs. Those who consistently express gratitude become gratefully minded beings through self-osmosis.

Start out by acting on your waking-thoughts exercise: Write a note to one of the two people who helped you yesterday. Keep it short but heartfelt. Better yet, put in a phone call so that your tone of voice will help to communicate to the receiving party what a difference he or she has made. If practical, deliver your thanks in person. Don't accept "it was nothing" for an answer, either. People have trouble accepting thanks sometimes, but they need to accept others' gratitude to reap its rewards.

Begin meetings at work with a statement of gratitude to the other parties involved, especially if you've been working together for some time. Think of it as the "what's going right" section of the meeting moved to the front. This is a far better kickoff to a discussion than a list of gripes. This frames meetings as gatherings of kindred spirits, which can lead to cooperation and collaboration.

Dr. Martin Seligman, the father of the modern positive psychology movement, suggests that you take it even further with what he calls "a gratitude visit." Here's how it works: Think of someone who has helped you, been kind to you, made a difference in your life—but to whom you've never expressed your thanks. Write a letter clearly outlining what he or she did and how much it has meant to you. Set up a meeting, and then read the letter to that person out loud. Make this the whole point of the visit, and give him or her a copy of the letter to keep.

When Seligman's students and patients at the University of Pennsylvania did this exercise, they were touched deeply by the experience. In many cases, both the letter's author and the receiver cried, moved by the spirit of gratitude. In some cases, the experience had a ripple effect, causing the receiver to think of someone in his or her life who had not yet been thanked and leading to a powerful gratitude visit to that person. And so on.[4]

Recently, adapting this concept to the digital era, I scrolled through my list of friends on Facebook, aiming to locate and thank someone from my past. I stumbled across Sam Bloom, the man who had hired me at Broadcast.com back in 1997. He took a chance on me and supported me when I had a slow sales start, and I have so much to thank him for.

He lives in Dallas, too far for an impromptu visit, so I wrote him a note, fully explaining how he'd changed my life and thanking him profusely for giving me a chance and some encouragement along the way. A few days later, his answer came back: "I helped you because you deserved it. I could tell you would take advantage of the opportunity, so I gave it to you."

This is the promise of gratitude expressed: Through positive feedback, you'll feel more capable, more deserving, and almost destined to be successful in life. This is the essence of the confident outlook. Keep gratitude locked up, and you'll convince yourself that either you are just lucky or you didn't deserve the help you received.

## TAKE YOUR GRATITUDE PUBLIC

At Yahoo! we had a bulletin board where coworkers could post notes of gratitude. At Citibank, employees fill out "World of Thanks" circular thank-you cards and send them to those they appreciate—often leading to cubicles adorned with words of thanks. At Cisco, engineers in one group dedicate a whiteboard in the commons for ad hoc shout-outs.

By giving public thanks, you inspire others, too. Culture is built by expressing values, communicating that "around here, we help each other and appreciate each other's help."

Here are a few ways you can use the Internet to do this. Visit www.TodayWeAreRich.com, post a public thank-you to someone on your list, and make sure that person is notified. You can use social media to do this as well, dedicating your status updates to thanking others for their contributions. A strong sense of gratitude will fuel your faith and extend your endurance in life. Gratefulness will push fear and anxiety out of your consciousness. It's a powerful cleansing agent for your psyche, dissolving any resentment, jealousy, and envy that clog your attitudes with emotional sludge.

Almost any negative thought pattern can be broken with thoughts of gratitude. When you "think thanks," you dial into what you have instead of what you lack. The effect is immediate—you feel positive.

One of Billye's favorite sayings is, "You can't be hateful when you are grateful!" She's right. You can't be negative when you're in giving-thanks mode. You can't be jealous of others when you are filled with a sense of personal abundance. Gratitude will improve your attitude and lift the altitude at which you fly in life.

Research also suggests that gratitude will boost your health and well-being. Robert Emmons conducted studies at the University of California Davis that tracked people who kept gratitude journals, like the one I suggested you start. He compared the gratitude group with a control group whose members didn't keep a journal of thanks.

In the study, the journaling group had fewer physical ailments, reported feeling better about their lives as a whole, and expressed greater optimism about the future. They had more energy, enjoyed better moods, and were more outgoing than those in the control group. That's the healing power of giving thanks![5]

Erwin McManus found similar effects in his ministry and wrote about them in his book *Uprising*: "Gratitude not only allows you to enjoy the present, but keeps you looking forward to the future. . . . Gratitude fuels optimism and inspires hope."[6]

When your gratitude muscle is strong, your total confidence soars. You see yourself as deserving on a human level. You recognize you have a community around you that wants to help. Your faith in God is bolstered, in which case it makes sense to account for what God gives you and include thanks for all of it in your prayers.

## TURN HAVE-TOS INTO GET-TOS

Perhaps the ultimate benefit of gratitude is that it gives you the freedom to frame your entire life as an exciting adventure, regardless of your circumstances. If you have a grateful mind-set, you can turn your have-tos into get-tos.[7]

Although many people complain because they "have to go to work today," millions of unemployed people would be grateful for a job—any job—to go to. Some parents gripe about all the things they have to do with their kids, and yet childless adults weep with longing and wish they could drive a daughter or son to soccer practice or cook for a loving family.

Gratitude, then, gives you the mental power to transform obligations into opportunities. It gives you the strength to transmute suffering into a growth experience. In some cases, this may be the only way you survive.

In 1992, Billye was diagnosed with breast cancer. When she told me the news, my heart sank. The prognosis called for immediate surgery to remove the lump, followed by multiple rounds of radiation treatment.

One of the nearest treatment centers was in Dallas, where Jacqueline and I were living at the time. So we picked Billye up and moved her into our house. When she arrived, her disposition was sunny, and she gushed with gratefulness for us. Each day, Jacqueline drove her to the hospital for radiation therapy, a treatment that can wring the very life out of a patient.

Billye withered, could hardly hold down food, and was drained of energy. Her skin had a gray pallor, and she could hardly walk. Most people in her situation become angry, sad, and listless. They may lash out at the loved ones caring for them. But Billye was vigilant, counting her blessings instead of compiling an inventory of her ailments. She was gentle with Jacqueline, even when she felt awful, and thanked her every day for driving her to the center.

I'll never forget one day that was weeks into her draining radiation program. Billye sat on the edge of her bed dressed as if she were going to church, slapping her hands together and saying, "I'm not gonna cry like Job, no siree! I've licked a lot of things before. Whipped them with prayer. This is my time to shine. I'm going to be the happiest patient they've ever had! I'll be a testimony to the power of faith."

Against the longest of odds, she lived with us for months, yet never had an outburst of negativity or grief. The secret to her misery-defying attitude was her well-developed gratitude muscle. It turned her have-tos into get-tos, even during her darkest hour.

Here's the way she saw it: She "got to" spend time with us and get to know young Anthony better. She "got to" experience world-class treatment that would help her lick the cancer. She "got to" witness to some new people she met at the center. To this day, she looks back on the experience with intense gratefulness for God, her family, the doctors, and all the strangers she met during that journey in Texas.

Billye's attitude likely saved her life by creating the right frame of mind for her to win her battle with cancer. She always looks back on it as a learning experience, with a little pain as the price of admission.

She insists that Jacqueline and I have enjoyed our

success because of what we did for her during that rough patch. Every time we visit her, she thanks us again and reminds us that she'll never forget how much we love her. Her gratitude warms our hearts and inspires us to find other opportunities to help those in need. This is the good loop of gratitude at work.

John F. Kennedy is credited as having said, "As we express our gratitude, we must never forget that the highest appreciation is not to utter words, but to live by them." If you feel fortunate, let it change you as a person. Turn this newfound energy into generosity. Gratitude will give you a desire to give back, so act on it, because when you give from a heart of thanks, you are ready to be rich.

# 7

## GIVE TO BE RICH

No matter how much you follow the first three principles, there will always be events in your life that are beyond your control. Financial difficulties, overwork, relationship issues, and personal tragedies can produce emotional wear and tear. Resulting stress, worry, resentment, anger, and sorrow can wear down your emotional resistance and cause your confidence to crumble. For these maladies, I prescribe the exercise of giving.

Giving is a wonder drug. No ailment can withstand its healing powers. Even heart disease can't beat it. As part of an experiment, a group of recovering cardiac patients at Duke University Medical

Center were asked to volunteer their time to counsel newly admitted heart patients. They sat with these new patients, listened to them, and offered support. Through the magic of giving, these volunteers recovered 60 percent faster than their nonvolunteering counterparts.

I've learned through my research on the subject that, by its nature, giving requires a focus on other people's needs, as well as on your assets. This redirects your mind toward strengths and away from weaknesses. In turn, the subconscious responds to this stimulus by deploying an array of chemicals and enzymes that change your mental and physical state.

From your work life to your family life, when you give to others, you receive a gift as well. Whether you are burned out, freaked out, or sad beyond words, a little time spent helping others can often lift you back up.

## BOOST YOUR WAY OUT OF BURNOUT

In our go-go-go lives, it's easy to run out of gas. Work can pile up with no stopping point in sight. At some point, the stress wears down our emotional shock absorbers, and we reach the burnout stage. This leads to a defeated attitude, a decline in optimism, and even depression. Jon Schwartz, former sales VP at Yahoo!, hit the wall in 2002. He was managing dozens of salespeople at a time when the company was struggling to make its numbers.

Every day, more than two hundred e-mails demanded his attention. He spent hours in meetings, worked through lunch to play catch-up, and flew at least twice a week to visit regional offices. The pressure for results was relentless, and progress was slow.

Jon hadn't had a real break in more than four years, and that was taking a mental toll on him. His bright-sided nature was fading as he struggled with nagging doubts and frustrations. Then he read about a program at work called Yahoo! for Good, a volunteer effort to install computers and Internet access at local schools in need. It sounded like a good alternative to the weekend e-mail marathons he usually conducted, so he volunteered.

On Saturdays, he stood shoulder to shoulder with his coworkers, creating workstations, installing computer terminals, and showing youngsters how to use the World Wide Web for school. These activities had an invigorating effect on him.

"Every time I feel beat-up from work, I just show up the next Saturday to help," he told me. "Physical exhaustion, especially for a good cause, is the best way to quiet the mind. It can send us back to work with the clearheaded, problem-solving, getting-stuff-done sweet spot we all crave."

According to Allan Luks, researcher and author of *The Healing Power of Doing Good*, Jon's experience is quite common. In his research, Luks studied thousands of volunteers and discovered that they achieved a "helper's high" that was very similar to what a person experiences after a long run. It's a euphoric feeling that, unlike "runner's high," lasts for several weeks.[1] Luks also found that volunteers who later reflected on their giving were refreshed by doing so.

In some cases, burnout is a consequence of task repetition over time. Do the same thing long enough, and you can lose your love for it. Dentists experience burnout as a result of years working in stressful environments. The American Association of Cosmetic Dentistry came up with a solution: Give Back A Smile. This program matches volunteer dental professionals with female victims of physical abuse who need cosmetic dental work as a result of that abuse. I spoke with several dentists who gave their time to this program, and each one told me how the activity reinvigorated them and put them back in touch with why they had chosen their profession. These feelings spilled over into their workweeks as they were able to reconnect with their patients—and with the difference giving them a smile can make.

When people tell me they need a break, I always recommend a giving break instead of a doing-nothing break. The positive feedback that surely follows a time of giving will do wonders for their points of view as well as their energy levels. They'll soon find that the best way to refresh their spirits is to give a sip of joy to someone in need.

> **One of the best ways to refresh your spirit is to give a sip of joy to someone in need.**

## ERADICATE THOUGHTS OF LACK AND WORRY WITH A GIFT

Not-enough-ism is a scourge of the psyche that can paralyze you with worry. When you think you lack enough money to pay the bills, you can't think of anything else. Of course, in some cases, the shortfall is real, and you need to get busy and do what you can to remedy the situation. In many cases, though, the shortfall is a matter of perspective, and you don't have the right one. You've thought your way into a tizzy. You fret and panic for no reason and put pressure on yourself that's undeserved.

Before you let thoughts of lack become dominant,

challenge them through the act of giving. If the lack can survive the giving test, you'll know that your scarcity is real. For example, in India, those who consider themselves on the brink of poverty are encouraged to take to the streets to find a less fortunate family than theirs and give them their food and clothing.

This exercise helps those who feel they are poor to realize that they are better off than they thought. As one Indian teacher explained it to me, "The next day, when these givers gather for their meal, they see their surplus, not a shortage. The fact that they do not starve demands they rethink their situation. At that point, they realize they were suffering from the illusion of scarcity, a self-imposed nightmare."

One shortfall that can drain our confidence is the perceived lack of time. As we take on more responsibilities, we develop a creeping dread that at some point we will run out of time and fail. The more we think about it, the more we obsess about it, counting the minutes we lose each day and getting more depressed about our overload. In this case, giving works its magic.

Stanley Marcus Jr. was a mentor to me, doling out life and leadership advice over lunches in Dallas. "When you think you don't have time for anyone else," he told me, "challenge that thought by giving some away. Help an associate, and I promise you, you'll realize the next day that you have plenty of it, and renewed energy to catch up on what you missed."

Try this out in your life, too, the next time you don't think you have enough time to meet your goals. Give a little to someone who needs it, and don't forget to let it feed your energy and spur your creative calendar-management abilities. You will realize that time was owning you but that by giving it away, you took it back. This confirms what Nobel Prize–winning author André Gide once declared: "Complete possession is proved only by giving. All you are unable to give possesses you."[2]

Tackle all the apparent lacks in your life in this way. If you're thinking too much about your money problems, get creative and find a way to donate to a cause that lifts your spirits. Do you feel a lack of respect from others? Give some respect to someone who deserves it. Remember, your subconscious is easily directed by your actions, and giving what you feel you lack tells it there is a surplus after all.

## A RELIEF FROM GRIEF

Jay Beckley, a friend from Detroit, has a story that illustrates the medicinal power of giving. His son,

Myles, was born in 2002 and from the very beginning was special to everyone who met him.

"He was a gorgeous child with curly locks and a joyous smile," says Jay. "Wherever he went, he lit up the room. In prekindergarten school at Regis Catholic Elementary, he was an instant hit. He sang to a classmate, Maria, when she cried because she missed her mom. He pulled flowers out of the ground to give to his teacher, just to see her smile."

Jay took Myles with him often to the school's football practices, where he volunteered as an assistant coach. The players loved to see Myles on the sideline because he had a charismatic spirit. He'd charge around, waving his arms enthusiastically, firing up "Raider Nation."

On January 5, 2008, tragedy struck. Jay and his family were on a vacation in Costa Rica. At sunset, Jay, his daughter Theresa, and Myles were on a horseback ride on the beach when something spooked the horse Myles was riding and it took off with Myles on board. Because Myles's foot got stuck in the saddle holster as he fell off the galloping horse, he was dragged on the ground and sustained severe head injuries. The ambulance broke down on the way to the hospital, and an hour passed before Myles finally made it to the emergency room. That night, Myles passed away with Jay by his side.

"My first thought," Jay said, "was that I had failed my family, failed to look after Myles. I had let this happen. I was so disappointed in myself as a father. But then I realized that I still had a wife and two daughters to look after, and I needed to be strong. So I focused on what we would do to survive this."

Jay admits that right after the accident, he was furious with the horseback tour guide, who wasn't holding on to the reins on Myles's horse at the time of the accident. But in the moment when he decided to focus on being strong for his family, his negative feelings about the man dissolved.

"I didn't focus my energy on justice or blame," he explained. "That wasn't going to bring Myles back to us." When he saw the tour guide crying in the waiting room, he went to him and hugged him tightly. That gesture likely saved the guide intense grief and suffering. That was the first gift Jay gave during this process—forgiveness and release.

While Jay and Virginia were still in Costa Rica, members of his community back home were outpouring their condolences in the form of phone calls, flowers, and visits to the house with food.

"When my sister told me about this, my first

thought was that I didn't want my house to be one of those shrines to the deceased," Jay said. He didn't want pity; he wanted Myles back. When he shared this with the funeral director, he was advised to divert gifts to a scholarship fund in the name of Myles Beckley. The obituary notice requested that in lieu of flowers, donations be made to this fund to help a Detroit-area child in need to attend Regis Catholic Elementary.

About nine months later, inspired by the growing scholarship fund, Jay celebrated Myles's birthday with "Smyles Day," an event at the school. There was a Velcro wall for kids to climb, a bungee run, and other activities designed to bring cheer to everyone involved and to raise money for an annual scholarship.

"It's not just a fund-raiser; it is a cheer-raiser," Jay said.

Today, a bronze statue of Myles, with his trademark arms-in-the-air cheer pose, greets students on the playground. There's also a butterfly garden on campus honoring Myles's penchant for them. Smyles Day now has a charity golf component, bringing underwriters and more donors in to expand the scholarships to neighboring private schools and, soon, to less-developed countries.

"Through Smyles Day, we've found a way to

celebrate Myles's life," Jay explained. "I refuse to believe he's gone. Through Smyles Day, he lives on."

As Jay experienced the healing power of giving, he transmuted his grief over his son's death into a celebration of his life. He deflected pity and chose purpose. He found a way to substitute a smile for a frown. He also gave hundreds of other people the gift of giving too.

For Jay, the typical approach to such a crisis would have had even more tragic family implications. I explained to him that many grieving people put their energy into anger, blame, self-medication, and a rejection of their previously held values and beliefs. In cases like his, many parents spend their time prosecuting the responsible parties or wringing their hands and wondering why God would let this happen to them.

"If I did that," Jay said, "I wouldn't be in this house today, with my job, my health, and my family. My faith is my anchor, and today, we are stronger than ever."

Earlier in Jay's life, he had battled drug addiction and alcoholism. If he didn't have the purpose of Smyles Day and a focus on love and celebration, his response to Myles's death might have been far different.

After a long pause he speculated, "If I hadn't taken the approach I did, I might not be alive today."

When he said that, a tingle ran down my spine as I realized that it was a miracle that *I* was alive. When my father was murdered, I did not make the same positive decisions Jay did. I didn't *give* my way out of grief. I tried to hate, resent, and rebel my way out of it. I wasted my energy playing gumshoe detective, rejecting the principles Billye had raised me with and spreading my sorrow.

If you face grief and sorrow, please heed Jay's example: Take time to grieve in whatever way is natural for you, but then *forgive. Give. Love. Celebrate.* If only I had known this then, I could have avoided my sideways years.

## GIVING YOUR WAY TO GENEROSITY

Like gratitude, generosity is a spiritual muscle. When you build it up, you possess the strength to give freely and, with enough development, to be free from an inordinate attachment to possessions or status. When we don't give the generosity muscle attention because of our possession-oriented culture, it grows flabby. That is why some people have fleeting moments of generosity and yet on a day-to-day basis remain self-centered.

Regardless of how confident you become, you'll need to have a strong sense of generosity if you're going to be able to let go and share with others. Think of the rich man who doesn't believe in charity and obsesses with getting more, more, and more. He may be confident in his ability to earn, but because he lacks the spirit of generosity, he'll never be able to fully share. Although he'll have worth on paper and in the present moment, over time he'll fade away. Ralph Waldo Emerson often gave this stern warning to his congregations: "Without a rich heart, wealth is an ugly beggar."[3]

The exercise of giving can bulk up and tone your generosity muscle. But producing lasting results requires a thoughtful regimen. In other words, giving requires a sense of acumen. Give with the wrong intentions, and you'll either quit before you make a difference or, even worse, offend the person you are trying to help. Give in the wrong way, and you'll be disappointed and left with less desire to give in the future.

Each one of us has likely had a situation in which we bungled an attempt to give. Maybe that attempt wasn't a good fit for us, or we weren't ready for the complications that came with it. Perhaps we feel, in the end, that we were taken advantage of. Whatever the reason, we ended up wondering why we had tried to help in the first place. Much like a business failure, a giving bust hurts. A poor giving experience can cause us to doubt our own judgment or resent others. It can injure our spirits and set us back.

Billye's father, Tommie, once told her, "There are right ways and wrong ways to give. In most cases, the difference lies in the motivation behind it. Always scrutinize the why behind the what." He learned this the hard way, as he attempted to share his wealth with others. Over the course of his life, he refined his giving strategies just as much as he did his business tactics.

Here are four rules for effective giving.

## GIVE AS A REFLECTION OF YOUR VALUES

Have you ever bought a shirt on impulse and later decided it didn't mesh with your personality? Likely it was on sale or you were sucked in by a glitzy promotion. Eventually, though, you still had to donate the shirt all the same.

In giving, we face similar situations. We get involved in a cause with gusto, only to watch our interest fade as we realize that particular cause wasn't a good fit for us. We make a pledge in response to an emotional pitch; then when it's time to renew our commitment, we ignore the reminder because we don't have a strong connection to the cause.

The reflection test is a foolproof way to pick the right giving opportunity: When you consider contributing in some way, ask yourself, *Does the cause I'm considering reflect my values?* Our values define who we are and can be a source of great energy and creativity—they are the emotional center of our being.

Before you can give as a reflection of your values, you need to *identify* your personal values. Think of them as the priority list for how you spend your time and invest your resources. Think of them as your fundamental sense of right and wrong in this world. Identifying your values may take some time if you haven't already considered them explicitly. Take out your journal and write down five things you value in yourself and in other people. Write down five things you wish there were more of in the world. That's a good start. Now, rank each item on a scale from one to ten, with ten being a supervalue.

You now have a starting point for identifying the compass you'll use to say yes to some opportunities and "that's not a good fit for me" to others. Later, during the purpose principle to follow, this ranking of personal values will come in handy.

Sometimes our values emanate from a personal

experience. Other times values become important to us because they are the source of our success or happiness. For example, I value debate as a way to improve one's chances at success. It helped pay my way through college. It wasn't easy for me, though, because I lived in a rural town with an underfunded speech program. We didn't have a big library like those in college towns. We had to raise money to go to national tournaments. For many in my situation, it was impossible unless they went to a private school in Houston or Santa Fe.

A few years ago, I found out about the National Association for Urban Debate Leagues (NAUDL), a nonprofit organization that brings debate-team resources to inner-city, at-risk high school students. It funds teachers, summer camps, and transportation to tournaments. Students who participate in it are much more likely to earn their high school diplomas, attend college, and avoid poverty. What a direct hit considering my values!

As a reflection of myself, I give to this nonprofit. When I see its progress as it expands into new urban areas, I get even more excited and want to give more. This is the magic power of giving as a reflection of one's values.

If giving is a way to soothe the soul from grief after

a death in the family, where do we start? Jo and David Clark asked themselves this question in 2004, when their nineteen-year-old daughter Sally was killed by a drunk driver outside Charlotte, North Carolina. Sally was a freshman in college and very popular, an inspiration to everyone who knew her.

The Clarks, much like Jay Beckley, decided not to focus their energies on getting revenge on the drunk driver. Their spiritual teachings challenged them to find a way to somehow transmute their loss into blessing. They wanted to create something positive to remember their daughter by.

"What we didn't want," Jo told me, "was a billboard memorial. That wasn't good enough." They instinctively knew that Sally wouldn't have wanted celebrity. Instead, she would have wanted her life and death to have meaning.

About six months after the tragedy, David had a dream that revealed the solution to him. When he awoke, he told Jo, "I've got it! I know what we'll do. Sally valued fitness of body, mind, and spirit more than anything. Let's build a YMCA in East Lincoln in her honor."

David's dream revealed this connection to him. First, Sally loved physical fitness and being outdoors. Knee surgeries and asthma hadn't stopped her from taking on strenuous challenges, such as a mountain-bike exercise at a skill-building camp she attended. During the exercise, she had an asthma attack, yet she found the will to finish the course. This deeply inspired many of the kids and caused them to "think deeper about themselves."

"When she came home from that camp, I could see a real change in her," said her mother. "Fitness was something she wanted everyone to have. She loved to inspire others through her example."

Sally also held her faith as a core value. She loved singing at Grace Covenant Church and volunteering for activities. She talked about Christ often to others. She gave spare time to counsel other teens and encourage them.

The Clarks had been longtime YMCA members when they were younger. There wasn't a center where they lived in East Lincoln, so Sally didn't get a chance to enjoy its benefits the way they had. In the back of his mind, David always thought East Lincoln could support a center. When he recalled the YMCA's core values—"to put Christian principles into practice through programs that build healthy spirit, mind, and body for all"—he knew it was a match for Sally. It would powerfully reflect her in a way that would live for decades.

The Clarks had a huge task ahead of them. First, they had to convince the Charlotte YMCA that there should be a new center in their town of East Lincoln. The family offered the land for the new YMCA center and promised to embark on an aggressive fund-raising campaign to build and sustain it. They gave dozens of presentations, staged events in homes, and reached out to the media. They were persistent, creative, and most of all inspiring. By early 2009, they had raised almost seven million dollars, much of it during the doom-and-gloom economic environment of the times.

I met them over dinner the night before I spoke at a national YMCA leadership event. Jo was resolute about the center being a game changer in their community, inspiring others to grow from Sally's example. David was soft-spoken, but he had a twinkle in his eye as he talked about his experiences convincing others to donate to the cause. David and Jo, who are closer than ever, held hands through most of dinner. Their story is legendary in greater Charlotte, a testimony to how a family can make something good out of a tragedy.

The center is slated to open in spring 2011. It is appropriately named "Sally's Y."[4]

## GIVE TO EMPOWER OTHERS

When you give, you need to come from a place of humility, seeking to give to others what you want for yourself. If you give because you feel sorry for the needy, you are not empowering them. Think of it from the recipients' point of view: They don't want merely to survive; much like you, they want to thrive. They want the same opportunities you have. They don't want your pity.

In the 1930s, when Tommie King saw struggle in the local business community, he gave interest-free loans along with encouragement. He wasn't trying to put a bandage on the problem; he was attempting to forge a farming community. As Henry Ford, one of his heroes, often said, "Time and money spent in helping men to do more for themselves is far better than mere giving."[5]

Later in life, after the family bank fiasco had drained away his cash reserves, Tommie stumbled into a way to give unlimited power directly to other men in need. He learned the value of giving the invisible: wisdom, connections, and reputation. When he shared business know-how with a young entrepreneur, he created wealth. When he networked an opportunity with an ambitious person, he made magic happen. When he lent his sterling reputation to a business owner to help him get a loan, he became a money machine.

In each case, unlike giving cash, giving power didn't deplete Tommie's supply. In fact, the more he gave the power of know-how and connections, the more he had because of the feedback he received and the goodwill he generated. This jibes with the teachings of Daniel Lapin, author of *Thou Shall Prosper* (a fantastic book recommended to me by Dave Ramsey). Lapin told Ramsey that giving intangibles works like lighting candles. When you do it, you create more lit candles, not fewer. This is different from the pie-of-life point of view, where a slice given is a slice gone forever.

When you give to grow others' capabilities, you create abundance in their lives. No matter who you are, *you* can give power to people too. It's a matter of understanding what intangible value you have that's worth sharing. It may be your experience and the knowledge you've acquired. Over your life, you've built up a bounty of it. In the information era, all of us have a network of personal relationships. Many of the people in those relationships possess solutions for others' challenges. In other words, *your* friends may not have everything you need to succeed, but *their* friends do!

Whether you are helping someone on an individual basis or supporting an organized cause, aim to empower everyone involved. For example, when you decide to contribute to a nonprofit that reflects your values, don't stop at writing checks. Contribute your business savvy to help organizers improve at marketing or operations. Don't just lend money to friends who need help; tap into your network and lend your reputation to help them find new jobs.

Always look for an exit strategy to giving: At what point has the need been taken care of and the needy transformed into the self-reliant? Sure, when a crisis like Hurricane Katrina happens, be willing to pitch in right away to help the suffering get food and shelter. But, as actor Brad Pitt did when he created Make It Right New Orleans, aspire to make things better than they were before. His organization is building sustainable housing for flood victims. The goal goes beyond putting a roof over their heads—it is aimed at creating a thriving, growing community that will not need government support or donations in the future.

When you give power, especially to those around you, you create a more powerful world. When your giving empowers others, you gain more confidence in them and, in turn, in yourself. If you give others enough power, they will go beyond independence to possess material and intangible prosperity. This will allow them to go from being recipients to givers and make it possible for them to feel the joy and significance you feel when you get to help others in need. To quote author and philosopher John Andrew Holmes, "No exercise is better for the human heart than reaching down and lifting another up."[6] Pass it on.

## EXPECT NOTHING IN RETURN

A young man once visited Tommie King's office and asked him for advice on real-estate investing. Tommie spent the entire afternoon educating him about buying and selling land. Later, when he told a banker friend about what he had done, his friend asked, "Why did you waste your time on him? What can he possibly do for you?"

It's said that Tommie quipped, "I did it for the same reason the dog sleeps all day—because I like to do it, and because I can!"

That is the only way to give. When you give and then expect a return on your investment, you are an investor. When you give and expect public recognition in return, you are a self-promoter. But when you give only for the love of giving, you are a generous person.

Take the word *generosity*. It stems from the Latin

word *generosus*, which meant "of noble birth."[7] Over time, the word became associated with the spirit of nobility. The nobility gave to the poor because they enjoyed it and, most important, because they could. They had no expectations of receiving anything in return. This lies at the heart of what it means to be truly noble.

When you give, be careful to free yourself from any expectations of reciprocity. This will be a real workout for your generosity muscle because it stretches you to be free from attachments to your time or possessions. When you let go of those things and keep no accounting for their return, you are truly free.

A few years ago, while having lunch with an executive at a local company, I heard a familiar tale about a gift given and thanks not returned.

"Let me tell you why I don't give away my network anymore," the executive snorted. "People are happy to let you connect them, but they've forgotten about the concept of gratitude. A kid fresh out of college came up to me after I spoke at a conference. He had a software product and was looking for an introduction to some investors. I referred him to an outfit in Palo Alto, and before you know it, he'd secured funding for his start-up. A year later, his company launched. He'll probably end up richer than me in the end."

"Wow, what a great story," I said (great to me, anyway).

"You would think," he replied, "that he would at least come back to me and say thank you for getting him off the ground. You would think he'd appreciate what I did for him."

This story brings up an important point: When you expect gratitude from others, you will often be disappointed. In this executive's case, giving made him a less generous person because he had certain expectations and they were not met. I doubt he'll be free from attachment the next time he makes a business introduction or doles out advice.

No matter how hard you try, there will be times when you give and give and never get thanked enough. As long as you hold on to the egotistical notion that you should receive gratitude in return for your charity, you are setting yourself up to move backward in the development of your generosity.

In addition, expecting thanks is not a humble approach to giving. In many cases, our advice or introductions are only a piece of the puzzle. That's what I pointed out to this business mogul.

"So, the outfit you introduced him to—they funded the entire company?" I asked.

"Well, no, they initially declined, but eventually they became a minor investor," he replied.

"Did this entrepreneur need to build presentations, demos of his product, hire people, find a building, and secure his first customers?" I asked.

"Well, sure, but what's that got to do with anything?"

"Pardon me for saying this," I continued, "but what gives you the right to think that you made him a success? Why do you think that your singular act made all the difference in his company's launch?"

He admitted that he had never thought of it that way.

When you are in give-to-get mode, you usually don't.

Here's another reason we shouldn't expect reciprocity: The receiver may well be paying it forward. For all you know, your last charity case is out there giving it all away to strangers you'll never meet. So let it go so the next person can pay it forward.

Too often when people come into our lives looking for advice or help, we size them up in an attempt to determine their usefulness to us. We wonder what they can give us in return. This is a wrongheaded approach. We shouldn't screen potential recipients for their usefulness; we should examine ourselves to see whether we can be useful to them. We need to close our minds to any thoughts of how they could possibly repay us. We'll know we're getting it right when our recipients ask, "So, what can I do for you?" and we have no answer because we've never given it a moment's thought.

A great way to eliminate any expectation of getting something in return is to *give privately*. If you've ever had a secret admirer, you understand the power of discretion. You don't have to do anything about it; just enjoy the flattery! Too often, though, when we give, the public takes note. Buildings may be named after us, or our name is read on TV during the fund-raising campaign. True giving, the kind that will make you generous (i.e., "noble"), is something you'd do even if no one ever knew about it.

In 1972, a missionary and his family made a presentation at our church to raise money for an orphanage in Mexico. He showed slides of the kids, the village, and his church. We were the first of several cities he would visit in an attempt to raise about twenty thousand dollars.

He gave his presentation on Sunday morning and was planning to return as a guest pastor that evening. At the evening service, our preacher announced that the missionary was on his way back to Mexico to immediately proceed with the building of the orphanage. An anonymous donor at our church had written a check for the entire amount, plus an extra ten thousand for unforeseen expenses! It was a big mystery. Everyone looked around, wondering who the donor could have been.

Billye knew but was tight-lipped. Her best friend, Ethel, had recently inherited a fortune when her husband passed away. She hadn't known what she'd do with the money until that day. She asked Billye, who was a longtime supporter of our missions program, for advice. When she decided to write the check, she swore Billye to secrecy and asked the preacher to keep the donation private.

When Ethel was asked why she was making her gift such a secret operation, she paraphrased a portion of Scripture: When you give to the needy, do not let the left hand know what the right hand is doing, so that your giving may be in secret.[8]

Ethel further explained it this way: "By my secret, I'm free. Free from the burden of my wealth and of the world's suffering. Free from the need to size up this man's gratitude to me. Free from anything other than the joy of imagining the difference it will make."

Allow me to offer one cautionary note: Even though you don't expect anything, be ready to accept repayment if someone should try to repay you. Too often heavy givers pride themselves on always being "on top" of the equation with others. When they receive a token of appreciation from a recipient, they respond by giving even more. I heard one megagiver tell someone, "You'll never be able to outgive me!" This is not the way to think.

When you let others express their gratitude by giving back to you, you free them from their perceived debt to you. If you reject what they offer or escalate the situation with a new gift, you further enslave them. By denying what they offer, you assert yourself as superior to them. But when you graciously receive their gift, you make them equal to you. Another reason it's good for you to let others give back is that you'll experience the joy of receiving—the feeling that others can and will help you.

**GIVE ALL THE TIME**

Giving is like any other exercise: The more you do it, the better you get at it and the more you get out of it. You shouldn't do it on occasion, only in response to an emergency or on someone's birthday. You should do it all the time.

Of all Billye's charms, her gift-giving habit has been the most endearing. She always had a piece of butterscotch hard candy in her purse to give a child. She never missed the opportunity to give someone a compliment on his or her appearance, which meant it often took her ten minutes to exit a beauty parlor. When she learned of a congregation member's struggle, she was often the first to leap in and give assistance. "To all those who give all but come up short," she said, "I will be there. I will fill their valley with my love."

Whenever I really needed something, she quickly made sure I got it. "Every day is Christmas in our family," she told me. "I don't wait until the end of the year to meet your needs; I do it on the spot." Even though she was charitable at church and in the community, her family remained the center of her philanthropy. This afforded her the opportunity to practice it daily.

Givers give all the time not only to improve at it, but also because it's a must in the world we live in. The takers of the world are cunning, relentless, and creative in their efforts to steal from others. They work around the clock. We must be just as tenacious and just as willing to apply our talents for good.

First, much like gratitude requires, you need to *tune in to daily giving opportunities*. Listen to what people aren't saying to identify chances to add value or provide assistance. When someone is down, ask what's wrong and whether you can help. Spend idle "searching around" time to find ways to connect with your values and give. To get into this habit, use your journal. Every day, find three giving opportunities, no matter how small. Note each one, and commit yourself to acting on them by a certain deadline.

Next, *program giving into every interaction you have with others*. Billye's habit rubbed off on me in this regard. If you come to my house, you will leave with a gift. Invite me over, and I'll present one at the door. Have a conversation, and I'll attempt to share some knowledge or make a networking connection. I've always thought of this as a Southern-hospitality tradition, but really it's a way of continually pumping up one's generosity through repetition. Be creative, willing to let go of a possession a friend has complimented. Don't worry if someone sees the gift as inappropriate; you will learn from this experience and refine your giving ways.

You always have a gift you can give. *Always.* Rich, poor, secluded, exhausted—you should always be able to give when the opportunity presents itself. It's like breathing. If you are alive, you do it. To quote a Zimbabwean proverb, "If you can walk, you can dance. If you can talk, you can sing." It's a matter of opening your mind and staying committed to giving.

While serving as a chaplain at a Boston burn center, pastor Tim Kutzmark encountered a woman who exemplifies this point beautifully. Here, with his permission, is his account of what happened:[9]

*The night she came to the emergency room, no one expected Margaret to live. She was eighty-six years old, and the fire had ravaged so much of her body. She had been in the garden that day, raking leaves. She was known and loved for sharing the things she grew in her garden. Opening their door early on a weekday morning, neighbors would discover a fresh bouquet of daffodils tied with a small blue ribbon, or perhaps a beautifully shaped shiny red pepper.*

*"It wasn't really alive," Margaret would say, "unless it was shared."*

*The day of her accident, she was burning leaves in a deep pit in her yard. She slipped on the wet grass at the edge of the pit and then fell into the burning [pile of leaves]. Unable to get herself out, she lay in the smoldering fire for several hours until a neighbor discovered her.*

*As she was put on the examination table,*

*she started talking about her faith. One of her doctors remembers, "There we were, cutting off her clothing, preparing to put her in a drug-induced coma because that was the only way her body could perhaps survive the next weeks, and there she was, telling us about the love of God that was surrounding us. . . . I think we all worked harder to save her. She reminded us that we had gifts and strength and love to share. And share we did. We saved her life."*

*When asked about it later, this amazing woman commented, "I was raised to believe that you never went anywhere without offering a gift. . . . That night I was receiving such kindness from the doctors and nurses. They were holding me, helping me; in their own medical way, they were loving me. I wanted to give something back; I wanted to love them back. I can remember lying there on the table thinking, I've got nothing to give. In some way, that hurt more than the burns.*

*"But then I thought, there's always something to share. There's always a gift in everyone for every situation. And so I offered them what I had. I offered them my faith. I told them they were going to be held—no matter what happened—in a great, great power of healing and love. I told them*

*not to be afraid, but to trust however life unfolded itself at this moment. . . . And I shared with them until I could share no more."*

That woman's attitude is the essence of generous giving.

# 8

## PREPARE YOURSELF

During my sophomore year in high school, a thoughtful vice principal dropped me off at the speech and debate office, guessing the activity might suit my chatty personality. It involved fast talking and quick thinking, and there were trophies to be won. After one tournament, I was hooked.

I raised enough money to attend a debate camp in South Dakota the following summer. It was a research marathon, where about one hundred high school students assembled quotes, studies, and statistics related to our upcoming national topic.

Of all the activities related to debate, gathering and filing evidence was my favorite. Working with four-by-six index cards, color-coded dividers, and metal file drawers was seductive. For every few hours I invested, I could measure my progress by the inches of cards added to my collection. At tournaments, I needed a hand truck to lug around catalog cases of stuffed file drawers.

The first half of my junior year was a mixed bag of small-tournament victories and big-tournament defeats. I'd win the Roswell tournament but lose miserably when I faced private schools at the Albuquerque or Houston competitions. But these experiences only strengthened my resolve to win. After dinner each night, I'd spend hours and hours clipping, pasting, and filing index cards in an effort to catch up with the competition.

A few weeks before the Texas Tech Classic, a huge debate tourney held in February, Billye came into my room around midnight to give me some advice. She'd observed my obsession with evidence cards and my constant state of exhaustion.

"When the judges score you, do you get extra credit for having the most file drawers of evidence?" she asked.

"Of course not," I said. "They vote for the side that won the debate."

"Too bad," she said. "Because it seems like you've been working under that assumption."

"You don't understand debate," I said. "You need all these cards so you can prove your own assertions or counter your opponent's."

"Then let me ask you about this year's topic," she said. "It's about reforming the health-care system?"

"Medical care," I said, correcting her.

"Tell me this," she continued. "What is the history of medical care in the United States? Who built the first hospital? The first system of hospitals? What was the first medical school? What was the first medical insurance company?"

"That's history, not relevant to the policies being debated," I said.

"Just bear with me," she said. "What is the history of government regulation in medical care? What's worked the best? What always seems to fail?"

"Well, if you have a specific case, I might have cards on it," I replied.

"Here's my point," she said. "You are wide on medical care, meaning you are prepared with a surface point on all fronts. But you don't know the subject deeply. If you knew the history of medical care as well as the track record of regulation from day one, you'd have a frame of reference. You would be fast on your feet, able to tackle new ideas with your mind instead of with an index card."

That made sense to me. In several situations, deep knowledge would have helped me punch serious holes in the other team's cases and arguments, even without evidence cards. I realized that my limitation wasn't my local library's size. It was my commitment to really study the topic at hand.

Billye had one more line of questions related to my tournament preparation: "Why don't I ever hear noise coming out of your room?" she asked. "You give speeches and rebuttals at tournaments. You need to rehearse them in front of a mirror, pretending you're at a real tournament."

"I'd feel silly," I said. "There's no one here but me. It would be like talking to myself. Besides, we have practice debates every few weeks at school."

"Are you simulating real tournament situations to a tee or just running through your cases and responses?" she asked.

"It's a practice debate, so I guess we're just giving our stuff a run-through."

"When you were in the play at school last year, did you have dress rehearsals prior to the opening?" she asked.

"For two weeks before the first performance."

"Complete with costumes, props, and makeup?"

"Yeah, just like the real thing."

"That's a crucial piece of preparation," Billye said. "This way, your drama teacher could make technical adjustments prior to opening night. It also allowed all of you to get used to your performance surroundings."

"I get that," I said, "but debating is not the same thing as entertainment."

"But debating *is* a performance. It's really no different than acting, singing, or even selling something. When you don't rehearse 'as-if,' you'll likely be flustered when you are at a real tournament. As long as you continue to play with these cards instead of fully preparing, you'll continue to be disappointed in the results."

All those questions were starting to get to me, and it was now half past midnight. I felt as if Billye was being hard on me, so I went on the defensive. "I'm working harder than anyone else I know."

I remember her smiling and taking my hand in hers. "There's a mighty big difference between working hard and being willing to do the hard work required to prepare for your life's opportunities. The best prepared will always win. To be the best prepared, you need to do some things that aren't necessarily fun or easy."

The next morning, I woke up convinced my

grandmother was on to something. I needed to really prepare if I wanted to win. I spent the next week at the library, going deep in the U.S. medical system's history, from company to legislation. I didn't stop until I was a walking encyclopedia on the topic.

In my bedroom I rehearsed my opening remarks, then took the opposing side and gave rebuttals to those remarks. I convinced a neighboring team in Muleshoe to stage a series of debates with my team. We'd have an audience, a timekeeper, and a mock judge—just like the real thing.

When our team competed at the Texas Tech Classic, we beat a big-city school from San Antonio on the way to winning third place. I brought home a three-foot-tall trophy, which thrilled Billye.

In May, at the state tournament, we made it to the semifinal round, the best showing ever for a debate team from Clovis. Billye's system worked during my senior year and throughout college, helping me to win more than two hundred trophies during my debate career.

My level of preparation made me resilient when faced with adversity and proactive when shown opportunity. It helped me compete at a level that exceeded my wildest dreams—like a kid who goes from playing Pop Warner football to being part of a Super Bowl championship team. One of my child-hood heroes, Tom Landry, made preparation a sci-entific part of his approach to coaching the Dallas Cowboys. "If you are prepared," he told his players, "you will be confident, and will do the job."[1] There are different levels of preparation. In my case, I was approaching preparation tactically: gather resources, organize them, and practice my craft. That's likely how you approach your life's challenges, be they sell-ing, business, or social.

Your challenges are usually much deeper than your level of preparation. There are always unforeseen developments, extra efforts required to adjust, and a protracted resolution. These variables will sap the confidence from those who have done only surface preparation.

To be deeply prepared, you'll need to delve into your challenge, often tapping into a different part of yourself than you are used to. Deep preparation is strenuous and taxing. It will push you outside your comfort zone. To the outsider who's happy just to get by in life, it will look like overkill. Only the obsessive would go that far. That is why most people end up choosing to prepare at the surface level.

From the day I first read about Mark Cuban to the last day I worked for him, I respected his insanely deep level of preparation. He had a hard-to-achieve vision: be a billionaire entrepreneur. To do that, he'd need to create a successful start-up, take it public, and sell it to a top global company at the peak of a bull market.

In less than six years, he did just that with Broadcast.com. Along the way, he exhibited the deep-prep elements I'm about to reveal to you, the same ones that Billye admonished me to master when I was in high school. Cuban knew that most people wouldn't be willing to prepare as he did, and in the end, he emerged as one of the most successful businesspeople of the dot-com era.

Recently, for an article on success in entrepreneurship, Cuban was asked to share the best business advice he ever received. His answer is your challenge: "It came from Bobby Knight when I was in college [at Indiana University]. He said, 'Everyone has the will to win, but it's only those with the will to prepare that do win.' . . . The more I talked to friends, the more I realized how right he was. . . . As I started and grew companies, it became a core tenet of how I approached everything I did."[2]

Add to your existing preparation the following three elements, and you, too, will find the way to leap from good to great in everything you attempt.

## GET SMART

Abraham Lincoln is credited as having said, "If I only had an hour to chop down a tree, I would spend the first forty-five minutes sharpening my ax." While he likely learned this lesson during his time splitting rails, it was often reinforced during his political career. Like a newly sharpened ax, knowledge has the cut-through power to quickly move you from opportunity to achievement.

If you are starting a company, a job, a product, or a project, begin your journey by expanding your knowledge base relevant to the task at hand. In *Think and Grow Rich*, Napoleon Hill makes the case for this approach, based on his study of highly successful men such as Andrew Carnegie, Henry Ford, and Thomas Edison. He wrote, "Successful men, in all callings, never stop acquiring specialized knowledge related to their major purpose, business, or profession."[3]

This was my approach when I first went to work at AudioNet in 1997 (the company's name was later changed to Broadcast.com). While I had some general knowledge of Internet broadcasting and online marketing, I lacked a deep understanding of their finer points and connected concepts. So I crafted a get-smart program for myself, and over the course of three years I became an expert on all things Internet and marketing, which eventually landed me the role of directing the Yahoo! ValueLab, an in-house think tank.

Although our group was small, we were expertise enthusiasts, employing techniques I'm about to reveal to you. We briefed major customers, trade associations, and stock-market analysts from 2000 to 2003. We did deep research digs into potential marketing partners. In the end, we drove a quarter billion dollars of the company's revenue in 2002. Our specialized knowledge gave us the courage to predict and the ability to advise others on strategy. This group was not a pack of number crunchers with pocket protectors and slide rules. We were ravenous readers who loved to converse about theory, reality, and history. It was more like a graduate school study group than a data-mining operation.

To truly get smart, you'll have to strain yourself on many levels. You'll read more than you ever thought you would. You'll have to think purposefully about what you've read and digest it into nuggets of insight. You'll need to put yourself out there, discussing these nuggets with colleagues—and being willing to debate the issues. Often you'll have to employ creative powers, associating unrelated facts or examples to give new insights.

If you don't watch out, you can fall into the

busywork trap, where you pursue less mindful activities that seem to produce progress. In my debate career, clipping-gluing-filing evidence cards was my busywork. I felt as if I were doing my job, but it didn't require heavy mental lifting (which made my head hurt!). For the salesperson, busywork can include organizing leads or playing around in the sales-automation program. For the manager, busywork can be found in compiling or editing reports—from expenses to forecasts.

If you find yourself facing a daunting intellectual challenge and then resort to busywork to "give yourself a break," you are in this trap. And that's a shame, because if you were the smartest person on the team, you wouldn't be doing these chores. You would be

> **Ten hours of getting smart will yield the same value creation as forty hours of busywork.**

in charge of strategy. My own experience has taught me that ten hours of getting smart will yield the same value creation as forty hours of busywork.

## READERS ARE LEADERS

The first step on the path to getting smart is reading deeply. To do that, you'll need to commit a high percentage of your research time to reading books related to your job or opportunity. Up until now, you may have been in the habit of grazing—reading articles or blog posts on a given subject. That is surface-level research, and it gives you the same general knowledge that everyone else you know has. Reading books will take you much deeper into a subject.

Book readers are leaders. Many of the most successful executives I know are voracious readers. According to a 2007 Market Tools Survey I conducted, the average businessperson reads about one book a year related to his or her profession. The average chief (CEO, COO, CFO, etc.) reads six books in the same period. This is why your get-smart program will start at the bookstore and not with a search on Google.

Read books that help you fully grasp the "space" you are operating in. Think of your space as all the people, places, and things that occupy the industry you are in or the role you have in life. For example, I realized that the World Wide Web industry was a space where users were researching, communicating, and buying. That gave me a clue about how deeply I'd need to read to understand their attitudes and behaviors so I could anticipate future trends.

First I read all the top books that covered the

Internet, electronic commerce, and information technology. That gave me a baseline reference on the industry. Then I dove into marketing, advertising, branding, human behavior, and consumer shopping technology books.

To understand a business space, think of the industry or technology's history, successful players, economics, and the trends that influence success or failure. Look through your trade magazines or Web sites for book recommendations. Whether for professional or parental purposes, books can give you incredible insight. Visit your local bookstore and invest a few hours a month finding two or three new books that'll deepen your knowledge of your space.

As you read books, take notes as if you were still in college. In my first book, *Love Is the Killer App*, I called this the "cliff and tag" approach.[4] Billye taught me this when I was a child. When you see a great point, underline it, and log it along with its page number in the back or front of your book (on the blank pages). If you are using an e-book reader such as a Kindle or an iPad, this is very easy to do. Later, you'll be able to employ this approach for quick review or for sharing with others.

At some point, you'll feel like a walking encyclopedia on the space you are in. Look at every new project, presentation, product, or business opportunity as a chance to read a new book. When author and marketing guru Seth Godin wrote *Linchpin*, he read more than one hundred related books along the way—even though he was already an expert in many areas.

About now you might be thinking, *Where will I find the time?* This is the number one reason we read in small bites. Carry books with you everywhere you go. You have time when you're in transit, waiting between meetings, eating alone, before you go to bed, and when you first get up. Cut down on Internet surfing, a few sporting or entertainment events, and idle gossip, and you'll find enough time to complete one great book every month.

With books as your knowledge foundation, dig into the data found in the footnotes and in highly specialized trade outlets to understand how theory intersects with reality. Learn how to differentiate good methodology from opinions so as to sharpen your sense of what constitutes "proof." Request data, reports, or primary sources from people you meet with, and read them down to the fine print.

When you deal with new companies, research them deeply to understand their history, business model, values, and current situation. Create a two-page brief with relevant bullet points, and confirm your understanding of each company by sharing your brief with them. They'll be impressed with the work you've done!

## NETWORK KNOWLEDGE

The second way to get smart is to network. At this point you've likely become an expert at work, and now you are ready to join forces with others to multiply your knowledge base. The starting point is conversation: Talk about the books you are reading, and share data you've discovered. Turn average watercooler conversations into think talks, which will often generate enthusiasm (i.e., confidence) in other people. The more things are changing, the more valuable your knowledge will be to others.

Create lists of books you recommend for others. When you make a presentation, give out your e-mail address, and offer a book list to everyone who contacts you. You'll find that others are happy to share their book tips with you, too. Eventually, you'll create a knowledge loop where you get dozens of book recommendations from others every month.

Form your own think tank or, as Napoleon Hill coined it, Master Mind group. Keep it relatively small, up to six people maximum, just like a college study group. Have a weekly or monthly meeting to discuss findings, great books, or knowledge gaps that need to be addressed. Focus attention on future scenarios and on how history can provide insight. Don't limit the group to coworkers; if appropriate, team up with industry colleagues or even with competitors.

## MENTORIZING

The last get-smart approach is what I call "mentorizing." This is the act of being a mentor to another person and having a mentor of your own at the same time. Stanley Marcus Jr. was a mentor to me because he could tell I was hungry for knowledge about business, retail, and marketing—and he thought he'd learn a little from the exchange. He's right, too; you always learn by teaching. Your mentee often brings real-world feedback to you or extra resources you didn't already have. Think of this as knowledge networking! (One other benefit of mentoring is that when you are sharing advice, you are reliving a success experience and driving your values deeper into your psyche.) This is why Mr. Marcus once told me that "you'll never get dumber by making someone else smarter."

To secure a top mentor, be aspirational and pick a champion, a top dog in your field. Billye often told me to hang out with and study under the champions, especially those who were outdoing me. "Success is not exclusive," she said. "In fact, it is highly contagious. If you seek out the successful and offer to help them, they'll take you up on it because it's lonely at the top. Later, they'll tell you everything they know to help you along."

You may need to trade some grunt work for a few classes with your champion mentor because if she's very successful, she's very busy and will probably take you up on your offer.

One surefire way to get mentorship is to go back to school. University of Phoenix provides deep education via online learning as well as through instructor-based classes. Lynda.com provides video and text tutorials on a wide variety of subjects. Professionals who invest time in adult education leap forward in their knowledge because of the structure a course provides, the fact that it isn't free, and their pride in completing or working through it.

Every year, improve your knowledge résumé through self-education. Otherwise, you'll have to claw, scratch, or repeat your way to semi-success in life. I'm amazed every time I talk to someone who scans and browses his way through life. I feel as if he quit studying the day he left college for the real world.

The secret to Stanley Marcus Jr.'s success as a businessperson lay in that he was hungry for knowledge until his last breathing day, not just during his college years. He wrote, "Where is it written that the joy of learning belongs to the first decades of life? . . . The stimulation of the learning process is more rejuvenating than any mythical fountain of youth."[5]

Get smart, and you'll possess childlike enthusiasm for your challenges. When conditions suddenly change, you'll have a deep frame of reference to call upon for an adjustment. When you have done your research, you'll feel intellectually ready for anything. The future will be familiar to you, as most of it is predicted in the books you read. Change will be your friend, the great equalizer.

**REHEARSE FULLY**

A rehearsal is commonly defined as a "practice session preparatory to a public appearance."[6] As I learned from Billye during my debating years, it involves careful consideration of your performance environment and audience. It elevates your preparation from the mechanical to the thoughtful.

You might be saying to yourself, *I'm not a performer, so I don't need to rehearse. Just practicing my craft is good enough.* This isn't the way to prepare yourself for success. Your life is a series of performances with an audience, in the context of circumstances.

Conversations, presentations, meetings, sales pitches, writing, and skilled tasks all occur, at some point, in a make-or-break live situation.

You've likely grown up hearing the phrase "practice makes perfect." While there's value in repeating a task or exercise to master it, practice doesn't make perfect when you face adversity or novel circumstances. I've seen well-practiced speakers crumble when their PowerPoint presentations don't advance or look right. I've watched salespeople who had practiced their pitches dozens of times get that deer-in-the-headlights look when someone interrupted their presentation with an objection. I've read about top rookie surgeons getting unraveled when something goes wrong in an actual operating situation.

Not wanting to rehearse is natural because rehearsing is hard! It requires more thinking, imagination, pretending, and planning than you're used to. In many cases it will require you to face your future—including the worst-case scenario. A full rehearsal will gobble up time and resources.

Practice, on the other hand, is easy and quick.

As long as you believe that practice is good enough for perfection, you will continue to fall into the run-through trap: You mindlessly run through your presentation, counting the number of times you complete it to measure your progress. In some cases, if you practice too much, you are more likely to stumble during the real thing because you've grown used to perfect conditions where there is no outside feedback.

To maintain confidence, approach every performance with a mind-set that you'll rehearse so fully that nothing will surprise you when you are onstage. I even rehearsed writing this book prior to sitting down and typing. It helps me organize my thoughts and helps me unblock myself and avoid the type-delete-type-delete pattern. So take the following advice beyond public performances and apply it to any task you perform.

*Rehearse your coming day at the end of your morning ritual.* This is what Aveda founder Horst Rechelbacher does every day. He calls it "rehearsing the future." I do this every time I have a hectic day or a complicated trip coming up. I call it "going through my dance moves." The more I think through what I'm facing, the more relaxed I can be when the time comes.

*Create an outline.* Many performances involve content creation and delivery, and that should start with an outline. I consider an outline a vital part of the rehearsal process. It organizes my thoughts and develops a linear approach to any communication event. It also allows me to clearly see where my thoughts are going.

I have a whiteboard in my office, where prior to writing a presentation, an article, or a chapter, I bullet-point my thoughts. I use my digital camera to record these whiteboard outlines. Then, often, I erase the board and redraw the outline. The exercise helps me see where I'm losing the logical sequence of my point.

Create your outline from the audience's point of view, following its thinking process. Nick Morgan, author and speaking coach, explains it this way: "Your goal in a speech is to lead the audience through a decision-making process to solve a problem it has and for which you have the solution. Let's be very clear about this: You're going to provide the solution, although you may well get the audience to fill in some specifics, but you're going to lead the audience to that solution by respecting and following its decision-making process."[7]

Think of the outline as the first rehearsal prior to the creation of the product you'll present. I include it here because a good outline is done in anticipation of the audience's emotions, preexisting notions, and time limits. Later, when you rehearse the performance, you'll be able to refer to your outline to make technical adjustments to its order and flow.

## STAGE A SIMULATION

The most effective type of rehearsal is a simulation, in which you perform in circumstances nearly identical to those of the live event. This starts with some research on your part. For any presentation, first gather information on the room, the lighting, the audiovisual equipment, and the seating plan. Arrange to rehearse in the actual room you'll later use, if possible. Use your visual aids just as you will in the live event. Recruit a few volunteers to be your audience. Bring a clock to rehearse your timing.

For a conversation or informal meeting, ask a coworker to role-play with you. Make sure to brief him on who he's playing, including his character's personality traits and what emotions the character might be feeling. If your partner is willing and time permits, reverse roles so you can experience the other side of the conversation.

The more effort you put into replicating the actual performance environment, the better prepared you'll be. When you are in the real moment later, the familiarity of it will allow you to relax and perform at your highest level.

Simulation works for technical procedures too. Doctors at the University of Rochester hospital simulate vascular surgeries and see a dramatic boost in positive outcomes during actual life-and-death situations. As one surgeon reported, "Nothing will boost confidence in yourself and your team like being successful in the operating room during a simulation."

No simulation is exact, however, so you'll need to employ your imagination to fill in the gaps. You've likely done this as a child, playing make-believe game-show hostess, football star, or actor. I did it often. I'd put *Meet the Beatles!* on the turntable in the living room and throw a concert, using our upright Kirby vacuum cleaner handle as a makeshift microphone. I visualized myself filling Dodger Stadium with my voice, and I could hear the crowd's roar after each track. I would even bow. Billye used to hide around the corner, watching me act and smiling to herself. Later, she credited my make-believe concerts with my lack of fear of performing in front of crowds.

Somehow we tend to outgrow this willingness to suspend disbelief about reality, reserving it for watching movies or reading novels. We think we are being immature when we pretend. That's a shame, though, because being able to pretend can be a powerful tool for you. The more you relax, imagine, and play a little, the more powerful the rehearsal experience can be.

## VERBALIZE IN FRONT OF THE MIRROR

If you are preparing for any communication performance and a simulation is impractical, conduct a verbalization of your content. Saying the words out loud helps you correctly gauge your timing and work through phrasing and delivery. Winston Churchill, Woodrow Wilson, and evangelist Billy Sunday all verbalized in front of a mirror, looking themselves directly in the eye.[8]

In *The Magic of Believing*, Claude Bristol calls this the Mirroring Technique. Initially it works because it forces you to be your own audience and to believe what you are saying. "If you can convince yourself, you can convince the other fellow," Bristol wrote.[9] It's true. Think about the pep talks you've given yourself in the bathroom mirror during challenging times. Your conscious mind verbalizes to your subconscious mind, which often believes what you are saying and aligns your nervous system to support the message. The result is power.

Bristol continues, "It's what I call a supercharging method of stepping up the subconscious forces of the speaker so that when he appears before an audience those forces flow out to and affect his listeners."[10]

When you make eye contact with yourself as you verbalize your message in rehearsal, you become comfortable with facing one of your greatest critics—you. Later, you can easily achieve the same eye lock-in with others and produce a powerful gaze that exudes confidence. The result is often more receptive audience members who are willing to go along with you because they feel as if you are connecting with them.

Each time I have a speaking engagement, I employ this technique in my hotel room on the day of the event. I get up early enough to allow enough time for a verbalization of my entire speech; then I shower and dress for the talk. If I'm using slides, I place my laptop on a table underneath or near the mirror. I give the entire talk, holding eye contact with myself except when I need to advance slides. I imagine my audience, the room I'll be performing in, and even my stage. It's the Beatles live at Dodger Stadium all over again! Later, when it's time to give the talk for real, I don't get butterflies in my stomach. I'm ready to do it again.

The other benefit of the mirror technique is improved adaptability. Since I've activated my subconscious mind through eye contact, it can take over during the actual performance, thus freeing up part of my conscious mind to observe my audience's reactions and adjust the talk on the fly as needed in response to those reactions. Because I've rehearsed well, I don't

need to "think" to remember the next point or how
I should phrase something.

The mirror technique isn't limited to speeches.
It works like magic for meetings, crucial conversations, sales pitches, or even pick-me-up talks. If you
practice it enough, you'll find yourself automatically
falling into rehearsal mode as you brush your teeth
in the morning—and making casual eye contact
with yourself.

## VISUALIZE IN YOUR HEAD

The last type of rehearsal is visualization, which
occurs entirely in your mind. This is very handy for
procedures, techniques, or preparing for competition.
Sometimes you simply don't have the time or place
to verbalize in front of a mirror, but you can visualize
your presentation anywhere.

A mental rehearsal requires the highest level of
imagination to work its magic. You must conjure up
images of the conditions you'll perform in: the place,
audience, ambience, your appearance—everything.
The more vividly you see the images in your mind,
the more familiar they will be when you are live.

Several years ago, Dr. Judd Blaslotto conducted
a study at the University of Chicago that demonstrated the performance benefits of mental rehearsal.

He compared a group of participants who practiced making free throws to a group who visualized making the same number of free throws. At the end of the month, both groups had virtually the same level of improvement![11]

Today in the world of sports, visualizations are a critical part of preparation as coaches and trainers leverage their confidence-building power. The next time you watch the Olympics, if you look carefully, you'll see athletes closing their eyes before a ski run or a gymnastics routine and visualizing their upcoming performances.

## DON'T FORGET TO SET UP THE HURDLES

After Billye came into my room that night and gave me her advice, I began to rehearse my debate presentations in my room. Almost every time, though, just as I'd start to talk, I'd hear the vacuum cleaner start up in the adjoining bedroom. Finally, a few days before the Texas Tech Classic, I burst out of my room and confronted Billye for interrupting my rehearsal.

"Don't you know I'm rehearsing?" I asked.

"I'd like to introduce myself," she said, smiling and extending her hand. "I'm the janitor at the university, and today's the day I'm cleaning this here classroom."

She was making an important point: Conditions

will never be perfect. Sure enough, at the actual tournament, a school bell went off during my talk, proving her right.

Whether you're doing a simulation, a verbalization, or a visualization, don't forget to include obstacles and distractions in your rehearsal. When I gave my imaginary rock concerts as a kid, I had the crowd from "hello" and never factored in PA-system failures or a broken guitar string. Later in life, when I actually performed, I was ill prepared for adversity. I was rehearsing a fairy tale, not a real-world scenario.

An important part of preparation is to *anticipate objections to the points you'll make in a conversation or presentation*. Outline answers to overcome those, and separately rehearse presenting them to your skeptical audience member or conversation partner. The more you face objections during preparation, the more you'll be convinced that you're right, which will give you conviction when it counts.

A study released in the *European Journal of Social Sciences* made a breakthrough discovery: Teens who mentally rehearsed overcoming adverse competitive situations gained the most confidence in their ability to play soccer. This is called Motivation Specific Mastery (MS-Mastery). In this case, you visualize yourself actually mastering a challenging situation, not just running through it with a good outcome.[12]

For a simulation, instruct audience members to be realistic in offering objections or disagreeable body language. For a verbalization, don't turn off your cell phone, or better yet, turn on the TV (but keep the volume low). For a mental run-through, imagine various challenges to your presentation and how you'll overcome them. Don't create an unrealistically challenging environment, though; this is a rehearsal, not a minefield. You want successful rehearsals in order to have successful performances.

Distractions are the hardest things to prepare for. Ringing cell phones, fire alarms, people suddenly getting up and leaving the room—all of these can fluster you, regardless of how much you've rehearsed. So during your entire life, rehearse dealing with distractions.

For example, when you are flying on a plane and catching up on your e-mails, convert the crying baby behind you from an annoyance to an opportunity to perform with distractions. When you are in a meeting or talking and a cell phone rings or someone whips out his or her BlackBerry to check e-mail, treat it as an opportunity to practice ignoring it. This will not only prepare you better but also transmute distractions from negative experiences to constructive opportunities.

By including hurdles in your rehearsal process, you'll eliminate the element of surprise later when they appear during your actual performance. The objection will be launched, the distraction will occur, and you'll smile inwardly and think, *I was expecting you!*

Some time ago a friend shared a rehearsal success story: Stan Chen wanted to ask his boss for a raise. He'd been promised one for over a year, and he faced a difficult conversation that would either fatten his paycheck or cause him to quit his job. He picked his performance date: a car ride with his boss to visit a client in a neighboring town.

For two weeks leading up to this one-on-one with his boss, he rehearsed what he would say and how he'd respond to objections. To make it more realistic, he rehearsed as he drove his car to and from work. He asked his wife and later a coworker to ride with him and play the part of the boss. They peppered him with questions and put-offs, which helped him brush up on his answers.

When the day of the road trip arrived, Stan was calm and cool as he started the conversation. Sure enough, the boss had some objections, but Stan was ready for them and answered them crisply and confidently. In the end, he not only got a raise, but his boss was so impressed with him that he also promoted Stan to a supervisory position! Stan is living proof that rehearsal makes you ready for anything.

## FINAL PREP NOTE: MIND YOUR BODY

At this point, through research and rehearsal, you can be mentally prepared for life's challenges and opportunities. But, to quote W. Clement Stone and Napoleon Hill, "You are a mind with a body!"[13] In other words, you must take care of your body to get the most out of your mind.

Your mind has a host, a brain, that needs to function correctly for your mind to work. A lack of rest can tax your brain's capacity to distribute information correctly. That's why when you are burned out, you easily become emotional. Your brain begins misfiring, and logical function is inhibited.

When you don't feel well, your subconscious tells your mind that something is wrong and diverts your thinking to your physical condition. It puts a distracting set of thoughts into your consciousness, often producing negative emotions such as resentment or anger.

The night before any big challenge, do your best to get eight hours of sleep. You may need to rearrange your schedule, but if your performance is important, you can make the case. If travel places you in a strange time zone, I suggest taking a melatonin supplement with a half cup of water one hour before you need to fall asleep. Keep the room cool and set multiple alarm clocks so your subconscious doesn't wake you up constantly to "check the time."

Don't check e-mail after dinner. Don't put disturbing or thought-provoking information into your head before going to bed. Don't watch the news in bed. Wayne Dyer recommends that you fill your mind with positive thoughts such as gratitude and love and let the day's stress ooze out of you as you close your eyes.[14]

Don't stop at sleep, either. Give your mind a break every week by taking Sunday off. If possible, give yourself the weekend to enjoy family and friends. If you work seven days a week, you'll tax your brain to the point of exhaustion. You may be able to pull it off in your twenties, but eventually that work style will catch up with you.

Take a vacation every summer, at least one week. While you're on vacation, don't graze on work. Make all the necessary arrangements so you can completely unplug and forget projects, e-mail, and other pressures.

Finally, beyond being well rested, improve your

physical fitness with exercise and an active lifestyle. This was a big *aha* for me when I worked at Yahoo! In 2002, I flew more than half a million miles for work, and it taxed me greatly. I lost sleep, packed on pounds, and lost the pep in my step. Since my job had high mental demands, I exercised only my mind. When I added exercise and walking to my daily schedule, I found it easier to fall asleep. I felt bolder, and even the way I carried myself when I spoke changed.

When I originally talked to Eric Goldhart back in 2002, I ignored an important detail in his story: He had stopped going to the gym because he didn't think he had time for it. The first piece of advice I should have given him was to immediately go back to working out. Had he done that, he might have bounced back even quicker than he did. Eventually, as business conditions improved, he completed his regular preparation by getting back to his daily exercise routine.

If you are worried that all the sleep, exercise, weekend time off, and vacationing I've talked about will keep you from getting your work done, consider the benefits of being fully rested: You are alert, cheerful, and quick-witted. You are significantly less likely to catch colds and flu bugs because exercise enhances your resistance to disease. You are more grateful for your work and the lifestyle it affords you, and it shows in your attitude. You are emotionally resilient, able to shake off criticism. All of this will save you time—lots of it.

When you balance your preparation methods so that you take care of your mind *and* your body, you'll create an internal good loop. The healthy mind will send good chemicals to the body, which will cause it to relax. The healthy body will send good chemicals to the brain, which will enhance its capabilities.

The result? Faith and endurance.

# 9

## [ PRINCIPLE 6 ]

## BALANCE YOUR CONFIDENCE

When I was growing up, my neighbor Curt lived in a trailer park just down the road from our farm. He was my best friend in elementary school, and we spent most of our spare time playing together.

Curt and his brother competed in local Golden Gloves boxing competitions. His father coached boxing at the local gym, a dank facility in a basement underneath a flophouse on Grand Street. Curt encouraged me to join and train with him on Saturdays.

Despite my physical frailty, I was interested. I was determined to find a way to stand up to the bullies at school who constantly picked on me. At first, Billye was reluctant, worried that I might get hurt. But she also wanted me to have more confidence and reasoned that at our age, how much damage could Curt and I really inflict on each other?

Before my first visit to the gym, Curt's older brother offered to officiate a warm-up bout in their front yard. Curious, Billye came with me to offer encouragement. Kids from the trailer park gathered around as Curt and I put on leather headgear and adult-sized boxing gloves, which looked as big as pillows on me.

With a clang of the cowbell, the boxing match was under way. Curt danced around me, jabbing and weaving. Lacking any sense of coordination, I did my best not to fall over as I attempted to follow and avoid him at the same time.

Because I was tall and gangly, I stumbled around like a newborn foal trying to get its legs underneath it. I lacked any sort of grace, and when I tried to dance around, I looked as if I were dancing the Charleston. The kids in attendance howled with laughter. My biggest challenge was staying on my feet. When I took a wild swing, I'd lose my balance and fall over without even being hit.

The day before my first visit to the boxing gym, Billye gave me a lesson in physical balance. Until her teens, she had been a tomboy. She had attended charm classes as a teenager, which included techniques designed to teach her how to carry herself gracefully. One of her favorite practices involved balancing dishes on top of her head as she walked across the room. Thinking that would work for me, too, she collected plastic dishes and a cup and proceeded to give me a lesson.

I was mortified. I didn't need charm school, after all—I was about to rough it up with other boys, not with a bunch of debutantes!

"What does this have to do with fighting?" I asked her.

"Any sport requires coordination," she replied. "And to have that, you need a strong sense of balance. Your favorite wide receiver in football, Lynn Swann (of the Pittsburgh Steelers), took ballet lessons, and you can see how that worked out for his game!"

I nodded, recalling a television reporter talking about how football players of all types were studying ballet moves to gain added poise on the field. At first, they didn't want to do it either, but their coaches convinced them to give it a try. So should I.

"If you can cross the room with these dishes on your head and not drop a single one, you have balance," she said, and placed the trio of items carefully on the crown of my head.

At first I couldn't walk three feet without sending the cup and saucer crashing to the floor—and our dog running for the other room. But Billye coached me along, instructing me to focus on something, like the record player across the room, instead of on the items I was trying to balance on top of my head.

Eventually I made my way from one side of the room to the other with the plate, saucer, and cup perfectly balanced on my head. As I improved, Billye continued to preach balance to me and to relate it to my desire to learn to box.

"Balance gives you the ability to bob, weave, duck, and most of all, plant yourself for a powerful punch, just like Cassius Clay (later Muhammad Ali)," she promised. "Balance will make you a good dancer, in the ring or on *American Bandstand*."

We'd spent several Saturday mornings watching the smooth moves of the dancers on *American Bandstand* and *Soul Train*. I was envious of their stylish grace and smooth moves.

"Balance will help you in your thinking life too," Billye added. "From making dinner to making money, strike the balance. Every good recipe has just the right mix of ingredients. Every great executive has equal parts brains, guts, and desire."

Although my boxing career was short-lived, Billye's balance lessons continued. When I worked hard, she advised a little playtime to keep things even-keeled. When I involved myself in church activities, she counseled me to maintain my efforts in school. She encouraged me to mix arts with smarts so I'd be well-rounded.

During the 1970s, the self-reliance and self-esteem movements grew. To Billye, they seemed too centered on the concept of one's "self." A total focus on self, she worried, would keep us off-kilter and decrease our potential. Overfocusing on oneself wasn't balanced.

The books in our library taught people to cultivate three types of confident trust in their lives. Dr. Norman Vincent Peale, in *The Power of Positive Thinking*, pointed out that "the most powerful force in human nature is the spiritual-power technique taught in the Bible . . . faith in God, faith in other people, faith in yourself."[1]

Billye firmly believed that you had to believe in yourself first to have any type of positive thinking, but at the same time she knew that it wasn't the total recipe for confidence. When I joined the speech and debate team during my tenth-grade year, she made this point clear to me. At the time, I had a debate partner I needed to rely on, a coach I needed to believe in, and a set of challenges I'd never faced before—I was a kid from the country competing with big-city kids.

"Self-confidence is very important, but it's only the beginning," Billye said one day while she drove me to school for a tournament. "A rich sense of confidence comes from three different types of belief: confidence in yourself, trust in others, and faith in God." As I grabbed my filing drawers of evidence out of the backseat of our Buick Electra, she finished the lesson with a profound thought: "If you have all three kinds of confidence, you'll develop faith and endurance. When one kind of confidence runs short, the other two will be right there to refill it."

That's why she always said, "Today *we* are rich," when we had made a difference. Confidence is never about *you* alone; rich confidence also includes believing in the power of *we*. Total confidence requires a belief in yourself, other people in your life, and in something greater than yourself. When you possess all three of these beliefs, you'll have a balanced confidence—something that can sustain you through uncertainties and difficulties. Whenever possible, be aware of your level of confidence in each category, and fill up those that are running on empty. Now we'll look at what it means to have confidence in yourself.

## CONFIDENCE IN SELF

Stanford professor Albert Bandura spent several years studying the impact of students' self-confidence on their ability to learn and to finish tests. He found that confident students have a sense of self-efficacy—a belief that they are competent enough to successfully complete the task at hand. But where does this sense come from?

In his landmark book *Psycho-Cybernetics* plastic surgeon Maxwell Maltz pointed out the contribution of self-image to self-efficacy when he wrote, "With such self-definitions [I am dumb, I am poor in math, etc.], the student had to make poor grades in order to be true to himself. Unconsciously, making poor grades became a 'moral issue' with him."[2] In other words, when the report card came back with an F, the self-described poor student had proof that he was right! Maltz came up with this idea while analyzing why his patients continued to have negative views about themselves even after successful surgery to remove scars or disfigurements. He realized that many of his patients didn't need surgery so much as they needed a better self-image regarding their capabilities and strengths.

Fix the self-image, and patients believe they are good enough for love, success, or leadership, even without corrective surgery.

Maltz's book suggests that we continually improve our self-image so that our subconscious minds will actively pursue success. "The self-image," he wrote, "is a 'premise,' a base, or a foundation upon which your entire personality, your behavior, and even your circumstances are built."[3] Dr. Maltz went on to say, "Our Self-Image prescribes the limits for the accomplishment of any particular goals."[4] Based on your self-image, which steers everything, your mind is either your success mechanism or your failure machine.

In my own life, I've often found my self-image defining the boundaries of what I could achieve. When an opportunity came along that I didn't think myself capable of, I failed to seize it—every single time! As long as I declared myself incapable of being a good businessperson, I failed as an entrepreneur or manager, many times because I was sabotaging myself without knowing it. As Henry Ford has been credited with saying, "If you think you can do a thing or think you can't do a thing, you're right."

On the flip side, when you see yourself as up for the challenge, you gain the faith and endurance to complete it. That was the case with Richard Nguyen, a twentysomething tech-support specialist I worked with at Yahoo! Long before iPhones and BlackBerry PDAs seamlessly synced address books and e-mails with computers, more primitive devices such as the Scout introduced us to info on-the-go.

This metallic blue handheld device, the shape of a grenade, was given out to all attendees at a trade conference I visited one year. When I got to work the next day, I tried to install the Scout's software and load my laptop's data on it, to no avail.

When I requested assistance from our IT department, Richard was dispatched to help me. When I asked him if there was any hope that I could actually use the Scout, which would make my life more mobile, his response reflected his self-image: "I am the master of all things gadget. Always have been, always will be. I will get this to work if it's at all workable."

For two hours he fiddled with the Scout, my laptop, and various ways of connecting the two. He downloaded more software and then made calls to the manufacturer, as well as to our tech center in India. He was relentless, muttering, "You will not defeat me, Scout. I am the master of all things gadget."

Finally, with one last tweak, the devices synchronized, and Richard clapped his hands, exclaiming, "Oh *yes* I did!"

I now had a mobile device that contained up-to-date information, e-mails, and all my contacts. As I walked to the parking garage with my Scout in hand, I encountered a coworker who had attended the same conference and received the same device. When I asked him if he'd been able to install the software and get everything to work, he replied, "It's impossible. It doesn't fit with our PC's operating system."

Puzzled, I asked him which tech-support person he had worked with. "Bill, one of the old-timers," he replied. "Said it was impossible and would take a superhuman to figure out. Gonna ditch the device and wait for technology to catch up." Bill's self-image ("only human") led him to give up on the Scout instead of hanging in there long enough to figure it out.

Later that year, at an exclusive executive off-site meeting, I was surprised to see Richard in attendance. He was there as a personal tech attaché to our CEO, Tim Koogle. When I asked Tim why he had brought his own techie, he replied, "Don't you know? Richard is the master of all things gadget. He may be one of the most important people here!"

You have a self-image, whether or not you are aware of it. You have total control over it, and in the end you're the one who draws it up or modifies it.

Others may attempt to dictate how you should see yourself, but in the end it's your call. It's up to you whether you will steer your mind so that you live up to your God-given potential. You are the director and executive producer of the movie that plays in your mind. Make a good one.

## CONFIDENCE IN OTHERS

It's one thing to have appreciation or admiration for others; it's another thing entirely to trust them with your success. Confidence in others requires a high level of trust, one at which you are willing to let go of your control of a situation. We trust others because of the impressions they've made on us over time.

Although we might think we are being fair in our assessment of other people, often we subjectively choose to notice some details and ignore others. We have a filter of attention that we apply to our day-to-day lives, and it's through this filter that we generate trust in other people. We might minimize a coworker's success stories and maximize his or her failures.

To be more confident in another person, you need to make a conscious decision to be objective about how you picture him or her in your mind. This is a time to apply a modification of the golden rule: Assess others as you'd like others to assess you. If you want others to respect and trust you, then extend trust and respect to them as well.

Otherwise your rising self-confidence may empower your ego to become a ruthless judge of everyone in your life, operating with a mentality that proclaims, "If it's going to be done right, I will have to do it myself!" This will make you a Lone Ranger type who believes that no one else can perform at your level.

Regardless of how much self-confidence you generate, you can't succeed without help from others. If you insist on going it alone in life, your level of confidence will not be consistent because you'll find yourself up against forces you can't possibly overcome by yourself.

Billye often told me, "There's no such thing as a self-made man. There are go-getters, that's for sure, but no one person can move a mountain." In my experience, she's right—I've never hit a milestone in my life without having a group of people on my side. When I've tried to go it alone, I've always ended up on an island of despair with a sinking feeling that all is lost.

While I was working at Yahoo!, I witnessed this firsthand in a sales executive. He had come from the software industry, where he'd succeeded wildly on an individual basis. His successes had given him a strong self-image, but that didn't translate into a sense of confidence in his team during the dot-com bust of 2000.

If a deal was really important, he would step in and take over for the lowly salesperson, because he believed that only he was capable of closing it. If there was a problem with one of our products, he'd dictate changes to the development team instead of asking them for help. He operated the same way with the legal, PR, trade marketing, and even customer service departments. Over time, as the 2000–2001 recession set in, he started to lose faith that the company would be able to keep its doors open.

His attitude wasn't good for talent retention either. People don't like being distrusted. Some of the top sales staff fled to other companies, and others quit, even walking away from their stock options. The more this happened, the more the executive's fears were confirmed: We were doomed.

In 2002, he resigned, citing stress and burnout. He'd had enough of playing Atlas for a lifetime and couldn't bear to perform his job one more day. He also didn't believe that most of the dot-com companies we did business with would last, which fueled his sense of gloom and doom. The Internet community was supportive of Yahoo! and would have jumped at the chance to pitch in and brainstorm solutions for our lag in sales, but he wasn't having any of it because of his only-I-am-competent view of the world.

This is what happens when you try to go it alone. On the other hand, when you believe in your team, your confidence soars, even when you experience personal setbacks. With your team members, you are not alone in your ventures or struggles. You can then settle into a role of being a contributor instead of a savior.

If you lack confidence in your teammates in life, reread and then apply practices from principles 2 (Move the Conversation Forward) and 3 (Exercise Your Gratitude Muscle) to achieve balance.

As your confidence in your team increases, delegate some authority, defer some tasks, and then let go. When you do, make sure you offer encouragement. Clearly communicate that you believe in your team and that you have tremendous confidence that they will be successful.

Don't communicate your confidence just to your team; give yourself the same message. Visualize others in your life, be they coworkers or family members, as succeeding. See them producing high-quality results and even exceeding expectations. Paint a strong, smart, and talented picture of them in your mind. Expect them to succeed.

As much as your self-image matters, your image of others matters too. In psychology there is a phenomenon called the Pygmalion effect, which suggests that people respond to your expectations of them. If you think they've got courage, they'll sense that and possess it. If you see them as bumbling, they'll pick up on that and perform accordingly.

This is why leaders must consider confidence in the team strategic to the performance of the entire group. Visualize your team as a winning one, and see individuals as superheroes instead of zeros. Go to bat for them every day, and offer praise every chance you get.

## CONFIDENCE IN YOUR FAITH

Your faith is your belief in the strength of a higher power. It's your belief in the higher power's rightness and that as part of the grand scheme, you will be blessed in some way.

I speak often at business conventions around the world, where talking about spiritual things may not be appropriate for what I'm hired to talk about (technology, marketing, leadership, etc.). In those cases, I talk about an economic higher power: the Free Market. This is something everyone, regardless of religious beliefs, can agree on: Essentially, when it comes to business, good things happen to good people, and bad things happen to bad companies. There is a moral order to the way the world works. Why? One explanation is that ultimately the market takes care of its own, aided by media scrutiny, consumer activism, and regulatory oversight.

Adam Smith, whose work laid the groundwork for our understanding of capitalism, wrote that there is an invisible hand in the market that corrects everything so that the world is ultimately ruled by justice, fairness, and value. In the long run, evil never wins. That's how the forces of the market maintain its existence, much like a body fights off disease.

So, if you are running a business or selling a product and you are creating a worthy service or product, you should have faith that in the long run the market will reward your efforts. The history of capitalism supports you. Sure, there are times, like 1998, when bad companies like WorldCom or Enron broke the market's rules with impunity. But that was, as I like to say, "just the beginning of the movie." The ending, of course, was brutal for those same companies. For companies that put people above dollars, such as Southwest Airlines, SAS Institute, or Chick-fil-A, sustainable profits have come almost naturally over time.

In my case, my faith is in the God of the Bible.

This is how Billye raised me, often quoting Romans 8:31: "If God is for us, who can ever be against us?" This is where she got her supreme confidence, even in the face of losing her husband, her possessions, and many other things in her life. She knew that God was there for her. Absent this belief, she would have likely succumbed to human nature's tendency to crumble under extreme adversity.

We might think of God as the manager, the leader, or the ultimate authority. And although that's all true, Scripture also says that God cares for us as his creation. He wants us to be fulfilled in life. He wants us to treat each other with love and respect. That is why Scripture says, "God is love."[5] He wants to care for us as his children.

Whether in your business affairs or your spiritual life, having confidence in what's greater than yourself will create accountability. If you depend on God, as I do, or alternatively, if you believe the free market will take care of you, then you must play by the rules and be part of that plan, which is greater than your own selfish desires. This accountability is a hedge against people or organizations that can spin out of control.

Leaders who don't follow someone or something bigger than themselves will eventually become drunk with a false sense of their own power. In effect, these people are their own deities. The result in business is seen in companies like Enron. In religion, the absence of accountability spurs cults, such as the one led by Jim Jones in Guyana. In politics, it produces tyrants such as Germany's Hitler or the Pol Pot regime in Southeast Asia.

On the other hand, I've known countless business leaders who have faith in the free market and a healthy respect for its corrective powers. As a result, they proactively practice corporate social responsibility: They treat employees fairly, contribute to local communities, and conserve resources for future generations.

> **Leaders who don't follow something bigger than themselves will eventually become drunk with a false sense of their own power.**

In my Christian upbringing, I was taught that God looked after me every step of the way. My faith in the living God is the ultimate eternal insurance policy and one that I can never pay for. All I can do is believe and follow God's ways. This makes me accountable for going beyond mere self-preservation and acting as a follower of God by doing the right thing, giving back, and being an example to others.

When you believe that you have the support of

someone or something greater than yourself, your faith gives you the energy and enthusiasm you need to keep going. When you and your team have given all you can but still come up short, you can trust that you will get through it all. That is what we call a "miracle"—and people of faith look for those miracles. It's confidence in something greater than yourself that allows you to relax, put everything in the hands of that greater purpose, and get back to the task at hand. My personal belief in God allows me to do that on a regular basis.

When I was a young adult, Billye explained it to me this way: "When your faith is strong, you've got an extra tank of rocket fuel for those times when the road is long and there are no refill stations in sight." Over my life, I've found that faith gives a competitive advantage over those who believe only in themselves or their earthly capabilities. My faith gives me the ultimate support system.

For a lot of us type A personalities, letting go and putting a situation in the hands of God isn't natural for us. It feels wrong. We like to grab hold of it, figure it out, control it, and solve it.

Over the course of my life, I have heard countless stories about people who exhausted all human means in the face of adversity and responded by putting "their fate in God's hands." They let the outcome ride on their faith and put their minds on doing whatever they could to improve the outcome. In almost all cases, miracles happened, some great and some small. In many instances, when people trusted God, they were released from the heavy weight of the situation and were able to regain their focus and clarity.

One story, though, deserves special attention. It demonstrates that sometimes when you ask God for help, you'll get just the right advice for the situation. Recently my friend John Maxwell, an extraordinary business thinker, and I were talking about that human tendency to hold on tightly to our problems. John told me that in his early years, he used to struggle with leaving everything in God's hands. It wasn't because he didn't trust God; it's just that he trusted himself just as much. And he thought, like many of us, that if the problem wasn't something major, he really didn't need to bother God with it. He struggled for years with what the Scripture passage John 15:5, "Apart from me you can do nothing," meant.

"I had a whole list of things I could do without God," John told me. "And then one day, after a few years of internally wrestling with this issue, I came to the conclusion that when God said, 'Apart from me you can do nothing,' what he was really saying was,

'Without me, you can do nothing of eternal significance.' In other words, there are a lot of things I can do. But basically, they die. In the end, their value is minimal. They're just daily actions that are going to live for a moment, and then they'll have had their day, and we'll all move on. But the things that have eternal significance—the things that live on in the lives of people for years—I can't do those things by myself. I have to trust that what I am doing will be used by God. That changed my whole perspective on life."

John continued with a story from his early years as a church planter:

> We were in our first building program, and I was only twenty-four. It was a big building program for a kid who has never done a building program, period. We had dirt on our property—way too much dirt. There was no way to get rid of the dirt because we ran out of money. I sat on that clump of dirt, and I said to God in exasperation, "You're going to have to help me because I don't know how to get rid of all this dirt. I have no money. How am I going to handle this?" I can still remember how God spoke to my heart. He impressed on my heart something that made no sense to me. And yet I did it.

*There was a neighbor who did not like our building program and did not like me. God spoke to my heart, saying, Go ask your neighbor if he would like to have some dirt on his property. And I did, and he said no. And I went back and sat on the dirt pile again. And once again I heard, Go back and ask the neighbor. And I went back, and he said no. I went back to the dirt pile again. And once again I heard, Go back and ask the neighbor. Well, you know, I'm feeling a bit foolish by this time. But I did it.*

*When I walked on the man's porch, he looked at me and he said, "I said to myself, if you'd come three times, I'd let you put the dirt on my property." And on that day, as I walked off the porch, I understood that God's ways are higher than mine. I understood that if I wanted to do something truly significant, it wasn't a question of whether I should trust him or should give it to him. The question for me is whether I always trust him and always give it to him.*

If you feel as if your total support system consists only of people (your talent and your team's talent), then you won't have enough to carry you through the crises that will inevitably come—the situations that will stretch you beyond your abilities. You need to buttress your faith in preparation for those times. Principle 1 (Feed Your Mind Good Stuff) applies here: Feed your mind the big picture; read the Bible more often. If you are a business leader, you may want to read history books and note the rise and fall of companies that have depended only on their worthiness in order to catch a vision for that big picture. Apply practices from principle 3 (Exercise Your Gratitude Muscle) to increase your appreciation for God's power in your life.

The more you are willing to let go, relax, and put your future into God's hands, the more you will trust him implicitly over time. Sometimes your prayers will be answered with a no. This doesn't mean that you've been let down. It means that there are likely other factors you do not understand that require you to accept defeat this time. Don't let those times test your faith; let your faith test you and make you stronger.

## FOLLOW YOUR PURPOSE FOR AN EVEN KEEL

Now I'm going to shift the balance topic to a new place: your level of confidence. "There is such a thing," Billye once said, "as too much confidence. You get it when you are out of touch with reality. It will make you come across as conceited, putting people off. It'll cause you to ignore pitfalls and make big mistakes."

It's easy for our egos to generate overconfidence, especially when we receive the good loop's positive feedback. You see it with rising stars of all types, from the stage to the cubicle. After some success, they begin to think they are better than other people. Eventually, they alienate the very people who helped them succeed in the first place.

At the other end of the confidence spectrum is too much humility (otherwise known as false humility), demonstrated when we refuse to take credit for our accomplishments. We can have this individually or on behalf of our team. This false humility is often a ploy to garner approval from other people to whom we are deflecting the glory. Some people practice false humility because they think it puts them in greater favor with God. This distorts our view of what's working and can knock us out of the good loop by masking the positive feedback that steers us forward. Remember: Your subconscious is always listening in on the internal conversation.

To balance our confidence, we must find that sweet spot between its two extremes. This is hard to accomplish internally because our egos or our need to be liked distorts our perceptions. What we need is a tool that gives us a way to accurately level our sense of belief.

One of Billye's favorite tools was a foot-long bubble level. She used it to create straight lines for hanging art and building shelves. A decade ago, I bought a professional video camera and high-quality tripod. At the ball of the tripod was a small bubble level. When the bubble sat between the lines, the shot was straight. Without the level, you could drive yourself crazy trying to eyeball your way to accuracy.

Your life has a level that can help you balance your confidence. That level is your purpose. Think of your purpose as the lines between which you put the "bubble" to balance your confidence. A purpose is an effective focal point for your life, giving you a worthy goal to pursue in all your efforts. Once you've balanced your confidence, the need to be the best or to be well liked will take a backseat to your purpose—because opinions don't matter; results do. In other words, it's not about you, it's about your purpose.

Your purpose must involve something greater than yourself. Stanford professor William Damon defines one's purpose as "a stable and generalized intention to accomplish something that is at the same time meaningful to the self and consequential for the world beyond the self."[6] When you are living "on purpose," you make a difference to others, and that gives you a sense of meaning.

One of the foremost experts on purpose was the late Viktor Frankl, who wrote a beautiful book titled *Man's Search for Meaning*. This world-famous Nazi war camp survivor and psychiatrist suggested that we don't choose life's meaning but rather detect the meaning of life's moments. One of the ways we do this is by "creating a work or doing a deed."[7] In other words, as we are working to accomplish something, our purpose puts in an appearance, and hopefully we notice it.

How can you detect your higher purpose? It lies at the intersection of a make-a-difference opportunity and your personal capabilities. You recognize the outside need that your gifts can address, and a resulting sense of enthusiasm confirms to you that it is your purpose.

The best way to detect this intersection is to start with your gifts: talents, tendencies, abilities, natural skills, or instincts. Everyone has a gift, something they can contribute. The sooner you identify your gifts, the easier it will be to relate them to an outside need you care about.

In your journal, draw a vertical line down the center of a blank page. On the left side, write down a list of your talents: What can you do that's worth paying for? What "thing you do" makes a difference to the outside world? What do you as an individual bring to every situation? What God-given capabilities do you have?

Share this list with a family member or close friend to get an outside perspective. Be willing to add many items to this list so you don't miss out on the intersection. Include specific skills or general attributes.

Now, on the right side of the page, list needs that you care about. Think about what you've observed or experienced, what gets your blood boiling, or what brings tears to your eyes.[8]

Using this exercise, I recently refined my own statement of higher purpose. First, I summarized my talents, which included communications skills (writing and speaking) and marketing acumen. Next I identified the needs I cared about the most. These included fairness in business, dignity at work, and people's need to be loved by others.

In the beginning, my purpose was general: to participate in the ending of suffering. But while that gave me direction, it lacked the specificity I needed to guide my daily decisions. Then one day during a morning reading session, I stumbled across a Scripture verse that said, "Let us think of ways to motivate one another to acts of love and good works."[9] When I read it, I detected a purpose that was custom-made for my gifts: to motivate others to produce acts of love and good works. What a perfect fit for a motivational author and speaker! Because I'd done the above exercise in my journal, my mind was ready to detect and then select my purpose statement when it presented itself to me.

With this purpose statement in hand, I now have the lines to fit the bubble (my activities) in. If a business opportunity doesn't fit that statement, I decline. When I give a speech, I'm concerned only with the mission, not with being liked or achieving a standing ovation. When I wrote this book, I wasn't focused on winning awards or making money. Instead, how well I accomplished my purpose is the end-all measurement of my success.

To take your talents to a greater purpose, continue to ask yourself, *Why do I do this? How does this affect others?* until you've hit the outside need you care about. Ryan, a recent seminar attendee, used these questions to find his purpose. He said, "My talent is computer programming skills." When asked why that had purpose, he stumbled around the product's benefits, mostly financial, to the customer. But that didn't spark him to the point of purpose. Finally, he realized his programming skills were important because they helped him earn a handsome living with health-care benefits "to ensure his family's health and happiness." In his case, his purpose is providing for his family. They need him to be successful at work. That was my first adult purpose too, in my thirties, the one that got me back on track.

Mary Beth, another seminar attendee, had a different outcome. One of her talents was organizational skills, which helped groups or teams go from planning to execution. When she thought about why that was purposeful, she realized that she was promoting success both at her company (on which many relied for income) and at the breast cancer research nonprofit she served. Now she knew her purpose: to organize others for success!

Here's an important point: No one purpose is better or worse than any other purpose. If it's helpful to others and gives you meaning, it's the right one for you to follow. Serving your family or saving the environment—both are the right purpose if that is what sparks you and leverages what you have to offer.

You don't have to be original, either. You can subscribe to an organizational mission, such as your company's social pledge (to help communities, produce happiness for customers, and so on). You can support your life partner's purpose too.

You may have dual purposes. In my case, those are my family's health and happiness and my charter to promote good works and love. Whenever possible, I try to follow both at the same time—which can require creativity on my part. When I look at opportunities in this mode, I ask myself, *Can I do this and serve both purposes?* When the answer is yes, the bubble is squarely between the lines.

Your sense of purpose can change as new talents emerge and outside circumstances present new and pressing needs. A new father can find family purpose for the first time. A business executive might be drawn to a societal need on which his skills can have an impact. Here's a case in point: John Wood gave up his high-level position at Microsoft to create a nonprofit that promotes literacy in the third world. That decision wasn't the result of a midlife crisis on his part; it was an adjustment in purpose. He grew into it. For his complete story, read his book *Leaving Microsoft to Change the World.*[10]

## FOLLOWING PURPOSE VERSUS PURSUING PASSION

When I speak about the importance of following a purpose, some people ask me, "But what if I'm pursuing my passion? That's what the virtuosos and superstars do."

Parents, giving your children lifelong permission to follow their passions (self) instead of purpose (service) is bad advice. I know this might smart a bit, as the self-esteem movement started the "just follow your passions; don't let anyone tell you different" way of parenting. But that philosophy has produced millions of broken lives in which people drift aimlessly, doing what they want to do and not what they need to do to contribute to society. Later, when they finally abandon their passions, they realize that much of their lives were wasted chasing them.

For youth, pursuing passions helps them develop dimension and clarifies their natural talents and deep interests. But as we reach adulthood, we need to embrace the joy of service. The essence of spiritual maturity is when we begin to follow a purpose and enjoy, but not be governed by, our passions. When I was following my passion for music as an adult, my family suffered financially and emotionally. I was a job drifter, and we lived paycheck to paycheck without health-care coverage. Later, when I realized that my primary purpose was to ensure my family's health and happiness, music became a hobby, not the center of my life.

In my case, music was my passion; it wasn't my purpose. I did it because I enjoyed it. I wanted a record deal so I could play music full-time. If music had been my purpose (to bring joy to others), I would have approached my musicianship entirely differently.

The reason I had to make a conscious decision to make music a hobby, with budgeted time, has to do with the consumptive nature of passion. Self is a powerful force, and when passion strikes, nothing else matters. Often when we are involved with one of our passions, time flies and we experience a sense of flow. We can do the same thing for hours without being tired. All the problems of the world go away in the blissful moment of passionate living. You love your passion because of how it makes you feel, not the difference it makes. You are playing. Before you know it, you miss other obligations or forsake other opportunities in order to allow the passion to burn without interruption. This is why I never pursued a serious career until I found family purpose.

Many people advise you to do only what you love to do, asserting that any other route will lead to a miserable life. Helen Keller thought differently and wrote, "Many persons have a wrong idea of what constitutes true happiness. It is not attained through self-gratification but through fidelity to a worthy purpose."[11]

I'm not nay-saying what passion brings to performance. When you have an emotional connection to something, you have intense desire and energy. Here's the good news: Over time, I've developed a passion (desire and enthusiasm) for my purpose. While I've not yet found a way to use my music passion for my writing or speaking career, I have developed as much love for my career as I have for my music. The fulfillment that comes from following purpose will, as you mature, give you the best of both worlds and return you to the sense of flow and timelessness you had as a child when you played your favorite game.

## PURPOSE PRODUCES FAITH AND ENDURANCE

Purpose does more than keep your confidence on an even keel. It preserves it. James Allen wrote, "They who have no central purpose in their life fall an easy prey to petty worries."[12]

If you are aimless or selfish, any change in circumstance is unsettling. Your gut reaction will be *what does it mean to me?* Setbacks become personal crises, where you feel as if no one knows what you are going through. You are more sensitive to criticism from others. You lack any protection from anxiety. You find yourself easily discouraged and have a hard time finishing what you start. You lack inspiration.

Napoleon Hill wrote, "The most practical of all methods for controlling the mind is the habit of keeping it busy with a definite purpose."[13] When you follow a purpose, small problems pale in comparison to your mission. You can dismiss self-doubt and wave off personal uncertainty. Your cause is your shield, protecting you from naysayers and doomsdayers alike. Your mind is fixed on solutions, not on petty problems.

Your cause will also boost your total confidence. Because you are trying to make a difference, you'll have an internal sense of worthiness. You'll feel as if you deserve to be successful in your efforts. When you are faithful to a purpose, you'll have a sense of personal integrity. It will help you believe that others, and God, will be there with you. You'll feel connected to something greater than yourself, and through that connection, you'll feel more powerful.

As you live on purpose, small accomplishments will give you meaning, and that will produce spiritual adrenaline. Through a life of research and personal experience, Viktor Frankl learned that meaning is one of our greatest needs, and when it's fulfilled, we can endure any type of suffering with dignity.

In my own career, purpose gave me unlimited energy both physically and mentally. I first detected my professional purpose when I read *Being Digital*, a best-selling business book by MIT professor

Nicholas Negroponte. In it he predicted that information technology would create an open future where we would all be empowered to influence the companies we did business with and the politicians who served us. The book made a case for a digital future in which we'd consume information anytime and anyplace on computers or other devices—all part of a new world that would be more environmentally sustainable. It was also a place where the bad guys would always be caught, much quicker than in the past. By the end of the read, I felt a calling, a purpose: promoting the information age. I believed it would change the world for good, creating opportunities for millions of people and creating an age of transparency that would bring the bad guys of the world to justice. At work, my purpose animated me. I started sifting through my coworkers to sniff out the other true believers, who were as excited as I was about the coming of the Internet. I would form loosely based Master Mind groups, with the goal of helping companies of all types realize the potential of the Web to extend their business opportunities. We exchanged book recommendations, ideas from recent trade show presentations, and personal *aha* moments from our work in the field with clients.

This purpose fueled my confidence in myself

and my colleagues. Soon my desire to tell the world about the Internet revolution swelled. I sharpened my presentation skills, giving Monday-morning talks to my fellow salespeople at work in the "Crows' Nest," a public conference area above our cube farm at Broadcast.com. My audience grew each week, and eventually it included engineers, clients, and business partners. One day, business guru Tom Peters even populated my morning audience.

Ultimately my purpose helped me to redefine myself not simply as a salesperson but as an Internet evangelist, taking upon myself the task of mentoring every one of my clients on how to leverage the info revolution as an opportunity, not a threat. Every meeting with a customer was another opportunity to advance the Internet revolution.

Later, as chief solutions officer for Yahoo!, I flew more than one million miles between 2001 and 2003. I trotted the globe, missed meals, and lived out of a suitcase. There were fires to put out and deals to be cut. We were fighting for survival and at the same time building a global business. Because I felt that I was making a big difference in the world, hundreds of hours on planes didn't faze me. My spirits were high, and I joked around often to keep things loose. I remember those times as fun, not hard.

Since then, I've employed my purpose whenever I need a boost. It produces an internal pep talk that is convincing and energizing. The next time you hit the wall, think about the why behind your what. See the mission, and picture yourself on a hero's journey to serve it.

# 10

# PROMISE MADE, PROMISE KEPT

On a sunny day in the fall of 2006, Don, the chief sales executive at the company where Stacy worked, asked her a question that changed her life: "Have you ever considered quitting smoking?"

"No. I don't think I can do it," she answered. She didn't see herself as the willpower type. She'd smoked for almost twenty-five years, and it was the dominant habit in her life. But a few days later at a routine checkup, her doctor asked her the same question. When she repeated her answer for him, he told her about Chantix, a drug that eliminates cravings and reduces the pleasure of smoking.

"When your big boss and your doctor ask you to

do something and then offer to be there for you, what can you say?" she told me in an interview.

Stacy made a promise to both men: She would quit smoking!

Although Chantix made the ordeal much less painful than she had imagined, quitting a decades-old habit in which she took seventy thousand puffs a year was hard.

"I used the visual of the calendar, starting with the day I quit. If I cheated, I had to start all over again with a new date. I didn't want to blow it," she said.

Stacy told everyone at work she was quitting, and soon she felt as if she had a full-fledged support team to help her. She realized that she'd kicked the habit for good when she took a vacation to Jamaica in February 2007. There were people smoking everywhere, and she was far away from her support system. And yet she never once thought about buying or bumming a cigarette the entire trip. This experience convinced her that she would successfully keep her word—for life.

A few weeks later, Stacy's doctor gave her a new challenge: weight loss. "You kicked smoking; let's kick overeating and lose some weight," he told her.

This time, Stacy wasn't timid in her response; she was ready. She enlisted help, set a goal, and used a visual (scales) to track her progress. She radically changed her diet. She stopped eating junk food and snacks. She worked out regularly. "You can cut out cigarettes, but you can't cut out eating," she said. "I knew this would be harder, but I knew I was stronger now. I believed I could overcome anything."

Within the year, Stacy had lost sixty-five pounds. This second personal victory successfully reengineered her self-image, converting her from an "I can't do it" personality to an "I can do anything" type of person. Her outlook changed too. She went from pessimism to optimism in areas beyond her personal life, including her career.

Next, Stacy set her sights on getting promoted from manager to director at her company. For years she had felt as if she was in a rut in her current job. She was more than qualified, and if given the chance, she would make a big difference in the company.

*You know what, kid?* she told herself. *You quit smoking and lost over sixty pounds, all in a year. You can do anything. What do you want, a promotion? Fine. It's yours for the taking.*

Stacy wrote a business plan to make the case and pitched it to her boss. When she learned a few weeks later that her proposal had been rejected, she was devastated. For a time, she considered quitting her job. Then, drawing from her successes with smoking and weight loss, she decided she would try again later. After a few months, she rewrote her business plan for her promotion and pitched it again. This time, her case hit home, and she was promoted. (As it turned out, her first attempt failed mostly because of bad timing. Had she given up on the promotion, she'd have missed her goal, not because she wasn't good enough, but because she was chasing it at the wrong time.)

Around this time, Pfizer, the manufacturer of Chantix, approached Stacy about becoming a spokesperson for the drug. She had called their 800 number after she quit smoking to thank the company for making such a great solution for her. Company officials loved her energy and secured permission to use her photos and testimonial for their starter kit for new patients.

A few months later, Pfizer reps asked Stacy to speak at smoking-cessation clinics, which she did on her own time. She shared her personal story, helping people find the courage to give up those little white sticks. Today, she looks back on the whole experience as life changing, beginning with a single promise she made—and kept.

When I asked her to rate herself in the area of "finishing what you start" on a scale from one to ten, a remarkable finding emerged. First, I asked her to rate the 2005 Stacy.

"On a scale of one to ten, I guess I'd give myself a four at that time," she said. "I was the type of person who would start a project and never finish it. Unfinished work and broken promises were the story of my life."

Then I asked her to rate the 2007 Stacy who quit smoking and was losing weight.

"By then, in general terms, I was up to a six," she said.

"Why the jump?" I asked.

"Quitting smoking helped me think of myself differently. I needed to prove to myself that I could finish something with a positive outcome, and when I quit smoking, I began to try to apply that to other parts of my life too."

When I asked her to rate herself today, she upped her rating to a nine. But this time, she didn't understand why there was a radical jump in her finishing tendency. Based on my research, I knew the answer: Stacy was in the good loop, with an ever-improving self-image.

When she quit smoking, she received positive feedback from people she admired and trusted. She got the same feedback when she began to lose weight.

When she applied her finishing skills to her work, she received even more positive feedback. Then Pfizer piled it on by putting her into a public-speaking role on behalf of the company, which brought her into contact with other people she could help. They gave her glowing feedback, this time about how inspiring she was, and that did the trick.

"Today I feel like no negativity can touch me. I feel that strong. Nothing can own me anymore, and nothing is impossible," she said.

Billye would say that Stacy "raised her roof," her potential, by showing some resolve and keeping a hard promise. Around our house, there was no greater accomplishment one could achieve. I was raised to believe that if you can finish what you start and do what you say you are going to do, anything is possible.

"Promise made, promise kept." Billye would use that statement to punctuate a conversation after she had followed up on a pledge she'd made to someone at church. When I wanted to quit pop choir at school because it was really hard, she said the same thing— and insisted I keep my word to my teacher that I'd hang in there for the year.

Of all the values Billye holds, integrity is tops. "That's all you've got in the end," she told me once. She's right, too. If you don't respect yourself, you cannot maintain your confidence, regardless of how well you follow all the other principles in this book. Nothing will inform you as a person more than your actions, specifically your promise-keeping ratio during your life. It defines you as either a truth teller or a liar.

This is why I'm finishing with this point: Keep your promises. Fulfill your commitments. Each time you do, you'll feel the same sense of personal victory that Stacy did. Finishing, especially when you face adversity or difficulty, gives you a growth experience in which self-image improves and, in turn, expands the limits of what's possible.

That is also why quitting a bad habit is an excellent way to jump-start your life professionally or even as a parent. Make a promise to give up something you enjoy that is bad for you. Keep that promise, and redefine yourself as a person with strong willpower and resolve. Self-image expert Maxwell Maltz explains why: "Our habits are literally garments worn by our personalities."[1] Whether they are good habits (remembering other people's birthdays) or bad habits (smoking), you wear them as a statement about who you are. Knowing you should stop doing something but not doing it changes the way you picture yourself.

The same is true when it comes to keeping your commitments. If you make commitments and later break them, you blur others' vision about the kind of person you are. And when you consistently start projects only to abandon them, you begin to think of yourself as a serial quitter of everything except your bad habits.

Even though you might forget a casual promise you made but did not keep, your subconscious mind remembers everything. Then in moments of challenge, you summon up a hunch: *I can't finish this. I can't finish anything. Never have, never will.* While that may be a vague feeling, it likely springs from unfinished business earlier in your life.

Think of your promise-keeping tendency as the storage tank for your rocket fuel—your sense of confidence. When you keep your commitments, you maintain your sense of integrity and self-respect and see yourself as a person who can be trusted. This will prevent any leakage of confidence from little quit-defeats. It will also keep you from receiving negative feedback like "we can't depend on you" or "you lack execution skills."

Napoleon Hill observed many successful men during his research for *Think and Grow Rich.* All of them had a strong self-image that was protected by a track record of keeping their commitments, even when doing so required herculean efforts. "There may be no heroic connotation to the word 'persistence,'" he wrote, "but the quality [of persistence] is to the character of man what carbon is to steel."[2]

Promise made, promise kept is an action principle, not just an admonishment to keep your word. If you want to become a consistent promise keeper, you'll need to be thoughtful about your promises every step of the way. There are usually three reasons that promises aren't kept: They are forgotten, abandoned, or undervalued. In each case, there are practices that can convert a broken promise into victory of character. I'll wrap up this chapter by talking about these practices.

## A SYSTEM FOR DELIVERING ON PROMISES

Successful entrepreneurs follow a system for creating, launching, and leading a business. The system starts with the selection of a business concept. Then a business plan is created and resources are gathered. Finally, the business concept is delivered in the form of products and services. The system is not a random process. Without it, entrepreneurs will struggle because they lack direction.

This same system is a good way for you to approach making promises. After all, just like creating a business, a promise must deliver results. The reason many promises aren't kept is that they are treated as randomly as idle conversation. My promise system has three components: making, planning, and delivering.

Chew on promises before you spit them out. Eighteenth-century philosopher Jean-Jacques Rousseau, author of *The Social Contract*, wrote, "He who is most slow in making a promise is the most faithful in its performance."[3] Too often making a promise is our initial reaction to a challenge or an opportunity. We hear about a problem, make a promise, think about it later, and then often realize we should have kept our mouths shut.

"I know a guy who can help!" leaps out of our mouth in conversation, usually before we've vetted this by checking with "the guy" in the first place. We think it's a speedy way to react, but in many cases, we end up failing to deliver any help. In the modern networking economy, we are quick on the click to connect people without really thinking it through sufficiently.

As a rule, it's a good idea never to offer a promise as a first response to a problem, challenge, or opportunity. Instead, with the promise materializing in your head, ask a few questions to better your understanding of the situation. Do some research; then, if you still think you can deliver, make the promise later. It'll keep.

This will be hard, because it's fun to be Johnny-on-the-spot. So think of this approach as a way of delaying gratification. You are trying to avoid making a mistake (an unkept promise). Abraham Lincoln advised, "We must not promise what we ought not, lest we be called on to perform what we cannot."[4]

Avoid making any promises in emotional situations, good or bad. I've seen numerous cases of happy talk, where promises have been made during moments of joy. It's easy to be generous when something good has just happened to you, such as a promotion, a windfall, or a significant accomplishment. Your brain is filled with dopamine and endorphins. You want to spread the joy, so you promise to help the less successful in that moment.

On the other hand, when we are under pressure, we try to promise our way out of bad situations. In many cases, once we emphatically promise to do something about it, our antagonist backs off (for the moment). But while we feel as if we've defused the situation, what we did really functioned more like

> **We must not promise what we ought not, lest we be called on to perform what we cannot.**
> **—Abraham Lincoln**

a snooze alarm—it just put off the problem for a while. When you feel any level of emotion, let this signal to you that you shouldn't make a promise until you've had a chance to level out. Two mistakes don't solve a problem.

Here's one final thought: Agreements are also promises, and sometimes you should just say no. Until now, I've talked about proactive promises, the ones we create and offer. Many of the promises we make, though, are reactive agreements. We are asked to do something, we agree to it, and a promise is born. We accept responsibility or take on roles. If we don't keep the commitments later, we are promise breakers.

When someone asks you to agree on a deliverable, be judicious about accepting it. Consider your qualifications. Weigh the time commitment. If you aren't clear on the requirements, ask questions. When you think you can't deliver, say no every time, clearly spelling out why you can't or shouldn't accept the offer or command. If you have to, show the asker your schedule, so he can understand how full your plate is.

Once you make a promise, document it. Otherwise it can slip between the cracks. You'd be surprised how often we lack any real accounting for what we say we will do. Saying later, "I forgot" or "I don't remember saying that" will not suffice.

When you are in a meeting, record promises in your notes. I always carry a journal to my meetings. At the top of the page I write down the meeting, date, and participants. Then I fold the page over so that half of the back page faces me. This is where I write down any promises I make. This system allows me to clearly record each promise without letting it get lost between the scribbled notes of a meeting.

After I make a promise, I send an e-mail to the person I made it to, reviewing what I said I'd do and asking him or her to confirm my understanding. Be very clear about the time frame for delivery, and set realistic expectations. Think about the accuracy that a weather forecaster seeks and be just as thoughtful. Copy other people who should be involved so they are in the loop too.

Determine what expectations your promise created for others. What does success look like to them? Are there any contingencies, or is this an unconditional guarantee? Are they going to tell others, thus creating expectations outside of your conversation? These are all important questions because expectation management is key.

When you don't meet others' expectations, you generate a disturbing emotion in them: surprise. If someone's expectations are too great, make sure to reset him or her as soon as possible. It's normal for your commitment to get blown out of proportion, but if you don't manage the expectations, you'll soon own them.

Once you've committed, you need to plan how to deliver. Start your planning as soon as you confirm your promise. If you've promised to do something with no timetable attached, consider it "due upon receipt." Norman Vincent Peale believed that "promises are like crying babies in a theater, they should be carried out at once."[5] If you can, deliver earlier than expected.

Put the delivery deadline on your calendar. Break down complicated promises into stages, and record due dates for each one. For example, if you promise to write an article for an industry newsletter, schedule the following stages: research, outline, draft, and delivery. That way, you'll be able to see when you might be running behind on delivery instead of having to pull an all-nighter the day before the deadline (and, consequently, putting out a shoddy product).

Finally, deliver the product of the promise directly to its intended recipient. If it was much more difficult than you imagined, internalize it and be cheerful. When you complain about the difficulty in keeping your own promise, it reflects on your poor promise-making abilities. You can often cancel out any goodwill this way and brand yourself as a complainer instead of a finisher.

Now you need to verify that you've met expectations and then close the loop. Any loose ends are still remnants of an unkept promise. Either you kept it fully or you didn't. There's no in-between. This system will help you refine your ability to make, manage, and keep promises over time. You'll find that the longer you use this system, the fewer promises you'll make and the greater your promise-keeping ratio will become.

## PRACTICE PERSISTENCE

Some promises are not kept because they are forgotten or ill-advised, and the system I've outlined will address both causes. Most of the promises we don't keep, however, are broken out of a lack of persistence on our part. They are abandoned because of their unforeseen difficulty. In most cases, though, this unforeseen difficulty is a product of our minds, not a reality. We tend to slap the "mission impossible" label on the merely difficult, and over time, fewer and fewer of our challenges seem doable.

Consider some of our greatest achievers who practiced and preached persistence. Benjamin Franklin said, "Energy and persistence conquer all things."[6] Thomas Edison has been credited with saying that many people who failed did so because they gave up without realizing how close to success they were. And even Albert Einstein reportedly stated that his success wasn't so much due to his intelligence as to the fact that he stuck with the problems he was working on longer.

All three of these achievers practiced persistence. Over time, they developed habits that increased their tolerance for "failure" to the point where quitting was a last resort. I've studied these men as well as many other tenacious souls and discovered a few ways all of us can increase our stick-to-itiveness.

First, when you reach the emotional quit point, grit your teeth and go one step further—one more attempt, one more day. Edison was right; in many cases, one more step would either solve the problem or advance you enough to see the finish line, which would produce a second wind. Sure, at some point your efforts may become futile, but make that point prove itself to you every time.

If you believe one more try is just another attempt at the futile, give it one more try anyway using a different approach. Take a different route to the finish line. Find out how someone else did something like this differently, and try that technique. Try out one of the ideas you dismissed earlier; what can you lose?

Connect with your subconscious for finishing power. Give yourself a pep talk using the mirroring technique. Look yourself in the eye and repeat out loud the original promise or acceptance speech. In many cases, you are missing a piece of information that would help you keep your promise or understand its scope. Your subconscious likely has it stored away and will cough it up when it's asked to help. Think of a time when the simple solution just appeared to you out of thin air: an idea, a fact, a technique. It came from your great hard drive, and you likely begged it to give it to you.

In some situations, you need a creative solution to overcome an obstacle. When we make promises, we often overestimate our quick creative capability and underestimate circumstances. Creative thinking can sap you mentally and physically. This is another situation where the subconscious can help.

British comedian and professor John Cleese found a way to put his second brain to work: He gave it an assignment and then went to sleep. He often got blocked while he was working on a movie script or a comedy sketch. When he felt as if he was hitting the wall, he set aside the problem and went to bed, instructing his mind to "get to work on the problem." When he woke up the next day, the problem was worked out. In many cases, there was no problem at all; he had just been exhausted and needed a good night's sleep.

There is a caveat to this technique, Cleese warns. The work must be done already, meaning you've done your research and made your best conscious efforts to solve the problem. You can't sleep on something as a way of putting off the heavy lifting. When you've done your waking best, your subconscious will do its part to fill the gap.[7]

I've used a variation of this technique to activate my subconscious mind. When I'm stuck on a creative problem, I step away from the computer, go outside, and putter. I rake the yard, mumbling the problem to myself, and then when solutions come to me, stop to write them down in my pocket-size journal. I putt a golf ball around in my backyard and let thoughts come to me. Both Hill and Bristol advised this approach, in which one performs a mindless task with mindful intentions. Through repetition and the ensuing relaxation, you connect with what Napoleon Hill refers to as "the infinite intelligence" housed deep within you.

Next, transmute the have-to into a get-to by

repositioning your challenge as a rehearsal for achieving your goals in the face of extreme adversity. When I say it's a get-to, I mean it's a rare opportunity for you to grow from the experience of finishing. If you pursue your commitments the way you chase your dreams, you'll someday realize how linked the two really are. Take a deep breath and tell yourself, "I will finish this difficult task to build up my character strength. Later, when I'm facing the impossible, I'll remember how easily I overcame this situation."

Finally, when all else fails you, recruit a promise partner. Much like when you're quitting a bad habit, the more people you tell about your promise, the better your support system will be. When you are sneaking a smoke in the parking lot, a good friend in the know confronts you about your promise to quit, and you put out the cigarette. Same goes for business promises: Your partner, direct report, manager, or longtime colleague can be there for you, giving you assurance or going Dr. Phil on you to ensure that you finish.

One benefit of having a partner is his or her perspective. Often what you consider impossible is merely hard. Sometimes your partner will point out an obvious solution that was on the tip of your consciousness. Your partner might also point out repercussions you haven't considered should you quit. In all cases, talking through your problem with someone else will give you a sense of community and produce a spurt of energy for another round of effort.

Treat the practice of persistence as one of the most important personal-development projects you'll ever take on. There is no greater asset than your sheer will to finish. Calvin Coolidge put it best when he wrote, "Nothing in the world can take the place of persistence. Talent will not; nothing is more common than unsuccessful men with talent. Genius will not; unrewarded genius is almost a proverb. Education will not; the world is full of educated derelicts. Persistence and determination are omnipotent. The slogan 'press on' has solved and always will solve the problems of the human race."[8]

## BE ACCOUNTABLE FOR YOUR WORD

In too many situations we don't think about the ramifications of quitting. We get into rationalization mode and begin to think that the promise isn't valid anymore because circumstances have changed. This is a form of denial. To master the art of keeping promises, you'll have to change your mind-set to assume responsibility when you set an expectation.

When you are willing to pay the price for breaking

a promise, you are being accountable. Over time, this accountability will instill a strong sense of responsibility in you, giving you newfound resilience.

When calculating the price of breaking a promise, consider only the source of the promise. Keep your promises because of who *you* are, not because of who *they* are. Don't weigh the importance of the recipient in your quit-or-keep-going analysis. This will create a cynical form of inconsistency in your personality. Many people have an integrity gap, defined by the distance they would go to keep a commitment based on the recipient's importance to them.

Think of someone you deeply respect. It might be an executive at your company, your pastor, or your best friend. You've made a promise to that person, and now it looks very difficult to deliver on. Will you give up? Not likely, because this person's opinion of you is so important that you'll endure great pain to keep your word.

Now think of a casual acquaintance or a front-line new hire at work. You've made a promise to him, and now it looks very difficult to keep. How far will you go to deliver? Is your quit point closer for the non-VIP than it was for the ultra-important person? This is the integrity gap you need to close. When you can honestly do this exercise and conclude that your level of persistence would be the same, you've transmuted promises into statements about you instead of commitments that are subject to review.

The next time you are about to give in or give up, look decades into your future and see Brand You. Will you be thought of as a person of integrity, someone who finishes what you start? Or will you be thought of as a quitter? Unfortunately, there is little inbetween, so you must seriously consider the price you will pay when you quit.

In many cases, you'll be surprised that the non-VIP has as much power as the VIP in creating public opinion about the value of your word. But again, you aren't finishing for those people; you're finishing for you. Your subconscious will always remember if you kept your word, and because your self-image is important, that's one audience you need to satisfy.

One way of being accountable to a bad promise is to keep it regardless of the price. You may have agreed to do something that has turned into a monumental task with very little to show for it once you've completed it. But do it anyway to make a point to yourself. When you experience some real pain, accountability will make you more judicious about making future promises. Your subconscious will store the memory, and when you are about to make the same mistake again, a pit in your stomach will convince you to keep your mouth shut or decline the opportunity.

A few years ago I went through this exercise and it fixed me. I was living in Silicon Valley, where almost everyone you met had an idea for a company. One buddy had a vision for a dot-com start-up, and I offered to help him write his business plan and find his first angel investor.

He was serious about his new business, so he took me up on my promise. From the opening sentence of the business-plan document to the extensive budgets and profit-analysis spreadsheets, he expected me to be there with him every step of the way. I had had no idea how much work it would take!

Finding an angel investor for an unproven idea in 2003 was also a challenge much greater than I had anticipated. I didn't do my homework on my buddy, and when my first few contacts did, they determined that he lacked the experience necessary to be trusted with millions of dollars. Although I wanted to back out of my word, I said to myself, *You have only one way out—follow up until he gives up.*

Dozens of meetings and countless hours later, my buddy finally dropped his idea and settled back into the comfort of his job. From that day forward, I've been very careful about making promises without fully scoping out the work required, as well as the viability of what I'm about to get involved with. Absent this painful experience, I might still think I could help anyone get a start-up launched.

If, after giving all, you cannot keep your promise, you must pay the price of discomfort and embarrassment. Deliver the news directly to the party or parties you made the commitment to. Don't hide behind e-mail or voice mail and let technology do your dirty work. Facing the other party directly will require you to sweat out real-time accountability. You'll likely get direct feedback that will sting, and the entire experience will give you motivation to avoid bad promise making in the future.

Excuses or blame will only compound the issue. State the facts, assume all responsibility, and issue a no-strings apology. Once you've made the decision to quit, do so with haste. Each minute you don't is a moment of untruth.

When you break a promise, even when it's as slight as asking for more time, offer to compensate. If you are going to be a week late on delivering results, take less pay or agree to a new promise to make up for it. If you are dealing with someone to whom you have multiple commitments, deliver another one earlier than expected. When you recognize that no broken promise is free, you'll have more firepower for your promise-delivery system as well as your sense of persistence.

One day in 2004, while sorting through a box of keepsakes, I came across a red second-place ribbon from a district championship track meet in Roswell, New Mexico. It was crumpled, and the edges were frayed. When I picked it up and held it in my hand, a memory came back to me in high definition.

Where I grew up, being an athlete was important if you wanted to have a social life in junior or senior high school. If you lettered, you were part of the in crowd. Being skinny and small for my age, I wasn't built for competitive sports. On top of that, I had a respiratory illness that earned me the nickname Wheezer.

During my eighth-grade year, I tried out for everything. While I was allowed to suit up with the football team, I never played a competitive down. I was cut from the basketball team at the end of the first week. In late winter I tried out for the track team, choosing the mile as my event.

Coach Hoy didn't need another miler; he already

had a champion in Buddy Hutto, who had easily won at districts the year before. But the team had a place for a second miler, so Hoy reasoned, *Why not let Wheezer be the other one?*

Although I could keep up with Buddy at the practice track for the first hundred yards or so, the rest of the mile was excruciating for me. Sometimes it would take me twenty minutes to complete four laps around the 440-yard track. No one seemed to care, though, and I was allowed to travel with the team.

I attended five track meets prior to the district competition, and in each one, I was lapped. As I finished the third lap, the rest of the kids would finish the fourth and final one, often coming in right on top of me. Embarrassed, I would stop running when the finishers did, trying to blend in and not be noticed.

At the Texico track meet, the scorekeeper ran to me at the end of the race and awarded me second place. Not wanting to admit I had only finished three laps, I instead celebrated and whooped it up. Coach Hoy walked over to me and said, "Wheezer, son, take that ribbon back."

Returning that ribbon to the official's table was a walk of shame for me.

The boys on the team didn't really like me much. No one likes a quitter, especially when the quitter is wearing school colors. I even picked up a new nick-name: "Three Quarters of a Miler." I was the butt of practical jokes that ranged from getting popped with towels in the locker room to being taped to the bottom of a bench with several rolls of athletic tape.

At the district tournament, one of the boys on the team thought it would be hilarious if he rubbed three fingers of Tiger Balm in the inside of my running shorts. Tiger Balm is intended to loosen up one's muscles by producing heat, and it's activated by sunlight. That afternoon, under a hot spring sun, I ran with my tail on fire.

The mile was the last event of the day. I got off to a decent start, hanging with the pack for half of the first lap. Then, as always, I started to run out of gas as the adrenaline faded. I struggled to continue, falling behind quickly as my run turned into a series of run, cough, walk, run, cough, walk cycles.

As I neared the end of the third lap, the rest of the runners passed me, finishing the race and concluding the track meet. This time, though, I kept running. I decided that for once, I'd finish the mile at a track meet. I could hear Billye's voice in my ear, repeating Napoleon Hill's charge: "A quitter never wins, and a winner never quits."[9] I figured the team could wait another ten minutes or so for me to run one more lap.

As I trotted through the backstretch, I purposely looked away from the grandstand into an empty field. I knew everyone was probably laughing at me, and I didn't want to see it. I just wanted to finish.

As I turned the corner and hit the homestretch, I heard a cheer go up from the bleachers. It was my teammates, all of them, standing on their feet, pumping their fists in the air, yelling, "Run, Wheezer, run!"

It was the fastest hundred yards I ever ran in my life. The harder I ran, the louder I heard them cheer. Two of the host officials pulled a finish-line tape across the track for me to break, and when I did, I collapsed on the track. I was heaving and gasping for air, and my knees had raspberries on them from the fall.

Despite my belief that the boys on the team were mean, that day they acted with compassion, a testimony to human nature. They streamed down to the track, lining up in single file to shake my hand or slap me on the back in congratulations. The shot-putter on the team, a boy twice my size, tossed me over his shoulder like a sack of potatoes and carried me to the bus.

I sat in my normal seat, the same seat the outcast kid always takes on the bus: the one behind the driver. Normally I rode alone, but on the way home from districts, our team captain sat next to me. He'd had a typical day—six ribbons, five for first place and one for second place. He was the quarterback of the football team and the most popular boy at school.

Halfway home he looked at me and said, "Hold out your hand." I was worried that he was going to play a trick on me, but I held out my right hand nonetheless. I felt pretty brave in that moment.

He pulled out of his pocket a crumpled, stood-for-his-only-failure-that-day, gonna-go-in-the-trash, second-place ribbon that said "District" vertically on it. He placed it in my hand, and then closed it with his.

"You made us proud today, Wheezer," he said, with a grin on his face.

I could only gulp in response.

"You showed everybody what you were made of. I want you to have this ribbon. This is for the one you had to give back in Texico. Here you go, winner."

When I attended my class's thirty-year reunion, I introduced Jacqueline to the guys I went to school with. Several of them told her about an experience they never forgot—the day that Wheezer kept on running. It had left a big impression on them and marked a turning point in my social life in Clovis. The same guy that rubbed Tiger Balm in my shorts ended up my right-hand man when I ran for class president five years later.

And here lies the unexpected benefit of finishing what you start, promise made, promise kept. You will win people over through tenacity. No matter what you've got against you, there's something in the design of sentient beings that responds to grit and determination in others.

If you are willing to keep your word, no matter how futile it might seem or how difficult it may be, you will win friends and influence people. You will convince the skeptics and convert your detractors into cheerleaders.

When I showed up at Yahoo! in 2000, I quickly built up a reputation for having a tendency to execute. At the time, that wasn't a given, as many people talked a big game but failed to deliver when things got tough. My ethic was likely inspired by a suppressed story from my junior high years—a story about a kid who came in last but went home a winner for finishing.

# EPILOGUE

*A First Step into the Good Loop*

Over the last few years I have gone on a journey, writing this book. I've plumbed much deeper into my family's story than I had ever dared before. To recollect Billye's lessons and what they've meant to me, I have had to face my circumstances: my troubled youth, my father's death, everything.

Along the way, I've come to some surprising realizations about myself, as well as about Billye. For the first time in my life, I think I understand the nature of my relationship with her, our unique bond. We are interdependent. As much as she has been my rock, I have been her clay, an opportunity for her to make a difference and *be rich*.

Every time I go back to Clovis and drive in from the airport, I pass the water tower in Sudan, Texas. This is the spot where I got a new mom, one who wanted me and loved me unconditionally.

Usually I stop and take pictures of it and reminisce. When I see Billye, I always tell her that I have just seen the water tower and how much I appreciate her for what she did for me. She always perks up at the mention of the subject. A few years ago, when I was talking about it to her, I said that the tower was a symbol of second chances—and she heartily agreed, adding, "For me, too!"

At the time, the meaning of her remark escaped me, but recently I finally got it: When I came into her life, she was battling through her own sideways years. In the early sixties, she'd fallen out of her spiritual practices and stopped feeding her mind good stuff, mostly as a result of her failing marriage. When she picked me up at the water tower, committing to raise me as her own, she took her first step toward the good loop by giving of herself. Over the next few years, she struggled to stay in it, her anger and depression bubbling up inside her as she lost her husband, her wealth, and later her two teenage boys.

The day she invited Clarence to step over the electric fence, she boldly stepped into that good loop

I have been describing in this book. With each step, she received signs that she was on the right path. First, she trusted a man to help her with farm tasks she couldn't do by herself. And it worked out just fine. That was a big step for her, given her recent betrayal. Next, she gave him twice what she had promised, likely most of her walking-around money at the time. And she felt great. That shifted her thinking from money problems to giving opportunities. Her serene faith that goodness would ultimately win gave her the foresight to see her life from what could be called an abundant perspective: "Today we are rich." Billye didn't have much at that time, but her actions led to a belief that she had enough—and that there would be enough in the future—to give of herself to others. That's the richness of life I saw that day as a kid and that I couldn't forget decades later.

As the years went on and as Billye taught me, she confirmed the principles to herself. Her morning confidence lessons in the bathroom were her way to recommit herself to those principles. As a kid, I saw these bathroom sessions as lessons meant for me. I realized later that Billye was also restating these lessons to herself in the mirror. She was reminding herself every day what was beautiful, good, and true. She lived each principle and taught me in real time. When she later battled breast cancer, those principles steadied her, preventing a spiritual relapse as a result of her physical suffering.

Today she's Miss Billye, cherished by everyone she spends time with. She has always got a good word for the day and expresses love to everyone around her. She's ninety-five years old as I write this, as healthy as a horse and as happy as a hound.

You see, by making a difference in my life and later noticing and accepting it, Billye entered the good loop of life. She's got rocket fuel, an endless supply of it. When I tell her about my books and speeches and we pray together, she relishes the fruits of her life's labor and thanks God for the blessings. She's not afraid of death, either. To her, the cup is full, and her life is complete.

This is a place I want to end up, a virtuous cycle, where I can make a difference to others and let the results continually refresh my soul and body. And I'm excited to know that it's possible, as long as I'm willing to faithfully practice the timeless principles Billye handed down to me. I invite you into this loop too. It's big enough for all of us.

◼

Billye always encouraged me as I was growing up to invest in the positive practices I describe in this book:

learning, thanking, giving, and finishing. Each one in turn led to positive feedback, such as recognition or a measurable success. This gave me confidence that I was doing what was right, so I did even more of it.

"Why do you think they call this the Good Book?" Billye asked me one night, tapping on her worn copy of the Bible. "Because it tells you to do good works, and when you do, you feel so rewarded that you want to do even more. And when you do, the whole process repeats again. That's the secret to living a good life!"

She called that "living in the good loop, a heaven on earth."

To paraphrase James, from the Good Book, "Faith without action is dead!"[1] The point is that living in the good loop requires that we act. Finishing this book will not be enough to change your life. Positive thinking is an outcome, not a prescribed behavior. It requires much effort and discipline. *It's a lifestyle decision.* I've offered you dozens of actions you can start doing today; the key is for you to single out one of them and take your first step into the good loop. Billye did that at the water tower in dusty Sudan when I was a toddler. Inspired by a photo of that water tower years later, I took that first step back into the good loop as well.

In my case, the first step I took was feeding my

mind positive material by devoting time each morning to the Bible and other great books. That practice immediately produced results and encouraged me to invest more time in adopting new principles being taught to me. One action, sustained over time, was enough to kick-start my ascent.

You need to do the same thing. Pick out one idea from this book and make a commitment, as Paula Cooper from chapter 6 did, to practice it for the next month. And don't keep it a secret project! Tell a friend or your significant other. Share your commitment with your boss. If you want, share it with me. I'd love to hear from you. Send me a note at tim@timsanders.com.

In going public with your plan, you'll have a support system that will help you follow through on your word. Who knows? You might be a positive influence on others when you share your personal plan for confidence. As you take those first steps, note how others are responding to you and how your life conditions are improving, and increase your time investment into living by the seven principles in this book. Now you are heading into the good loop, and if you stay here, you'll truly find a "heaven on earth" in your life as well.

# Notes

## CHAPTER 1: SIDEWAYS YEARS

1. To protect the privacy of the real subject of this story, I have changed his name. This allowed him to share more details with me for this book.

## CHAPTER 2: THE AWAKENING

1. Napoleon Hill, *Think and Grow Rich* (Rockville, MD: ARC Manor, 2007), 152.

## CHAPTER 3: THE GOOD LOOP

1. Norman Vincent Peale, *The Power of Positive Thinking* (New York: Fireside, 2003), 186–187.
2. I would define *total confidence* as a belief in one's self, in the others that he or she relies on, and in a higher power, such as God.

## CHAPTER 4: PRINCIPLE 1: FEED YOUR MIND GOOD STUFF

1. Napoleon Hill, *Think and Grow Rich* (Rockville, MD: ARC Manor, 2007), 40–41.
2. Claude M. Bristol, *The Magic of Believing* (New York: Pocket Books, 1991).
3. Maxwell Maltz, *Psycho-Cybernetics: A New Way to Get More Living out of Life* (New York: Pocket Books, 1989).
4. James Allen, *As a Man Thinketh* (New York: Jeremy P. Tarcher, 2008), 19–20.
5. Shawn Talbott, *The Cortisol Connection* (Alameda, CA: Hunter House, 2007), 110–112.

6. Maltz, *Psycho-Cybernetics*, 221.

7. Norman Vincent Peale, *The Power of Positive Thinking* (New York: Fireside, 2003), 160.

8. Tom Peters, *The Project 50 (Reinventing Work): Fifty Ways to Transform Every "Task" into a Project That Matters* (New York: Knopf, 1999), 13.

9. Maltz, *Psycho-Cybernetics*, 147.

10. In my journeys I have come across some wonderful morning shows, such as the *JB and Sandy Morning Show*, *The Gene and Julie Show*, and *The BJ Shea Morning Experience*, but they are the exceptions.

11. Maltz, *Psycho-Cybernetics*, xi–xii.

12. Ibid., 104.

13. Hill, *Grow Rich*, 159.

## CHAPTER 5: PRINCIPLE 2: MOVE THE CONVERSATION FORWARD

1. Ralph Waldo Emerson, "Circles," in *The Spiritual Emerson: Essential Writings*, ed. David M. Robinson (Boston: Beacon Press, 2003), 157.

2. Dale Carnegie, *How to Stop Worrying and Start Living* (New York: Pocket Books, 2004), 184.

3. William Shakespeare, *Hamlet*, act 2, scene 2.

4. For more on this idea, see Daniel Goleman, *Emotional Intelligence* (New York: Bantam, 2006).

5. Carnegie, *Stop Worrying*, 14–20.

6. Maxwell Maltz, *Psycho-Cybernetics: A New Way to Get More Living out of Life* (Upper Saddle River, NJ: Prentice-Hall, 1960), 77.

7. Kent Sayre, *Unstoppable Confidence: How to Use the Power of NLP to Be More Dynamic and Successful* (New York: McGraw-Hill, 2008), 116.

8. John Maxwell said this during his 2003 lecture at the Maximum Impact Simulcast.

9. David J. Schwartz, *The Magic of Thinking Big* (New York: Simon & Schuster, 1987), 45.

10. Ibid., 189.

11. Norman Vincent Peale, *The Power of Positive Thinking* (New York: Fireside, 2003), 120.

12. The training course referred to is called *The Dirty Dozen Rules of Email Etiquette*. For more information, visit www.EmailAtoZ.com.

13. Quoted in Geoff Garrett and Graeme Davies, *Herding Cats* (Devon, UK: Triarchy Press, 2010), 92.

## CHAPTER 6: PRINCIPLE 3: EXERCISE YOUR GRATITUDE MUSCLE

1. Maxwell Maltz, *Psycho-Cybernetics: A New Way to Get More Living out of Life* (New York: Pocket Books, 1989), 64.

2. Erwin Raphael McManus, *Uprising: A Revolution of the Soul* (Nashville, TN: Thomas Nelson, 2003), 125.

3. David J. Schwartz, *The Magic of Thinking Big* (New York: Simon & Schuster, 1987), 174.

4. Martin Seligman, *Authentic Happiness* (New York: The Free Press, 2004), 72.

5. Robert Emmons and Michael E. McCullough, "Gratitude and Well-Being: Summary of Findings," http://psychology.ucdavis.edu/labs/emmons/PWT/index.cfm?Section=4. Accessed October 26, 2010.

6. McManus, *Uprising*, 121.

7. I first heard this phrase from fellow author/speaker and friend Mark Schulman. Visit www.MarkSchulman.net for more information about him.

## CHAPTER 7: PRINCIPLE 4: GIVE TO BE RICH

1. Allan Luks and Peggy Payne, *The Healing Power of Doing Good* (Lincoln, NE: iUniverse.com, 2001), xi–xiii.

2. André Gide, *Pretexts: Reflections on Literature and Morality* (New Brunswick, NJ: Transaction Publishers, 2010), 310.

3. Ralph Waldo Emerson, *Ralph Waldo Emerson: Selected Essays, Lectures and Poems* (New York: Classic Books International, 2010), 272.

4. For more information, visit www.SallysY.org.

5. www.greatbusinessquotes.com/work_ethic_quotes.html. Accessed December 6, 2010.

6. John Andrew Holmes, quoted in Jon M. Huntsman, *Winners Never Cheat: Everyday Values We Learned as Children (But May Have Forgotten)* (Upper Saddle River, NJ: Pearson Education, 2005), 178.

7. *Cassels Compact Latin Dictionary*, compiler D. P. Simpson (New York: Dell Publishing Co., 1963), s.v. "Generosus."

8. Matthew 6:3-4

9. From his sermon "Scarcity and Abundance," given March 17, 2002, at the Unitarian Universalist Community Church of Glen Allen.

**CHAPTER 8: PRINCIPLE 5: PREPARE YOURSELF**

1. www.dailycelebrations.com/091103.htm. Accessed November 9, 2010.

2. Bianca Male, "Mark Cuban: Here's the Best Business Advice I Ever Got," *Business Insider*, May 19, 2010. www.businessinsider.com/mark-cuban-the-best-advice-i-ever-got-2010-5. Accessed November 9, 2010.

3. Napoleon Hill, *Think and Grow Rich* (Rockville, MD: ARC Manor, 2007), 60.

4. Tim Sanders, *Love Is the Killer App* (New York: Three Rivers Press, 2003), 79–82.

5. Stanley Marcus, *The Viewpoints of Stanley Marcus: A Ten-Year Perspective* (Denton, TX: University of North Texas Press, 1995), 32.

6. *Merriam-Webster's Collegiate Dictionary*, 11th edition, s.v. "Rehearsal."

7. Nick Morgan, *Working the Room: How to Move People to Action through Audience-centered Speaking* (Boston: Harvard Business School Publishing, 2003), 76–77.

8. Claude M. Bristol, *The Magic of Believing* (New York: Pocket Books, 1991), 104–105.

9. Ibid., 105.

10. Ibid., 104.

11. Joe Hoefner, "Mental Rehearsal and Visualization: The Secret to Improving Your Game without Touching a Basketball," www.breakthroughbasketball.com/mental/visualization.html. Accessed October 15, 2010.

12. Raweewat Rattanakoses and others, "Evaluating the Relationship of Imagery and Self-Confidence in Female and Male Athletes," *European Journal of Social Sciences* 10, no. 1 (2009): 129–142.

13. Napoleon Hill and W. Clement Stone, *Success through a Positive Mental Attitude* (New York: Pocket Books, 2007), 57.

14. Dyer recommended this practice in his 2009 PBS television special *Excuses Begone*.

**CHAPTER 9: PRINCIPLE 6: BALANCE YOUR CONFIDENCE**

1. Norman Vincent Peale, *The Power of Positive Thinking* (New York: Fireside, 2003), 88.

2. Maxwell Maltz, *Psycho-Cybernetics: A New Way to Get More Living out of Life* (New York: Pocket Books, 1989), 50.

3. Ibid., 2.

4. Ibid., 13.

5. 1 John 4:8

6. William Damon, *The Path to Purpose: Helping our Children Find Their Calling in Life* (New York: Free Press, 2008), 33.

7. Viktor Frankl, *Man's Search for Meaning* (Boston: Beacon Press, 2006), 115. Stephen R. Covey also discusses Frankl's "purpose detection moment" in *The 7 Habits of Highly Effective People* (New York: Free Press, 2004), 128.

8. Read habit 2 in Stephen R. Covey's *The 7 Habits of Highly Effective People* to develop your personal mission statement, or what Covey calls your "personal constitution." This will help you identify what you stand for or against.

9. Hebrews 10:24

10. John Wood, *Leaving Microsoft to Change the World: An Entrepreneur's Odyssey to Educate the World's Children* (New York: HarperCollins, 2007).

11. Dorothy Herrmann, *Helen Keller: A Life* (Chicago: University of Chicago Press, 1999), 261.

12. James Allen, *As a Man Thinketh* (New York: Jeremy P. Tarcher, 2008), 27.

13. Napoleon Hill, *Think and Grow Rich* (Rockville, MD: ARC Manor, 2007), 197.

**CHAPTER 10: PRINCIPLE 7: PROMISE MADE, PROMISE KEPT**

1. Maxwell Maltz, *Psycho-Cybernetics: A New Way to Get More Living out of Life* (New York: Pocket Books, 1989), 108.

2. Napoleon Hill, *Think and Grow Rich* (Rockville, MD: ARC Manor, 2007), 121.
3. Tryon Edwards, *A Dictionary of Thoughts* (New York: Cassell Publishing Company, 1891), 450.
4. Carl Sandburg, *Abraham Lincoln: The Prairie Years and the War Years* (New York: Mariner Books, 2002), 122.
5. Quotation included in *Crying: Webster's Quotations, Facts and Phrases*, ed. Philip M. Parker (San Diego, CA: Icon Group International, 2008), 2.
6. Blaine McCormick, *Ben Franklin: America's Original Entrepreneur* (Irvine, CA: Entrepreneur Media, 2008), xiv.
7. John Cleese discussed this idea in "De Bron van Creativiteit," a presentation to an audience in Belgium. It is available on YouTube at www.youtube.com/watch?v=zGt3-fxOvug&feature=player_ embedded#. Accessed on November 4, 2010.
8. Elizabeth A. Knowles, *The Oxford Dictionary of Quotations* (New York: Oxford University Press, 1999), 236. Quoted from a program at a Coolidge memorial service in 1933.
9. Hill, *Grow Rich*, 81.

**EPILOGUE**
1. James 2:20

# Acknowledgments

First and foremost, I am grateful for Billye King Coffman. Her life, her work, and her spirit make this book possible. I'm also appreciative of Jim Coffman, Michael Coffman, and Jan Bradburn for contributing details about our family story.

Thanks to:

Jan Miller, Shannon Marven, Nena Madonia, and Nicki Miser at Dupree Miller. This book was born in their Dallas offices.

Jon Farrar, Ron Beers, Lisa Jackson, April Kimura-Anderson, Maria Eriksen, and Susan Taylor at Tyndale House Publishers. What a great job you've done taking an idea all the way to a finished product!

Glenn Plaskin, fellow author and editor-deluxe. You gave me invaluable early feedback on the opening chapters of the book.

Gene Stone, my dear friend and mentor. All along the way as I wrote this book, I heard your helpful voice in my head, helping me make important decisions. Your influence on this work is profound.

Thanks to John Maxwell, Erwin McManus, Stacy B., Sande Golgart, Jay Beckley, Jo and David Clark, Tim Kutzmark, Paula Cooper, and Dave Ramsey for providing stories for the book. Thanks to my entire Facebook community (http://tinyurl.com/timpage) for all your feedback and comments during the writing process.

# About the Author

**Tim Sanders** is a sought-after international speaker, a consultant to Fortune 1000 companies, and the author of the *New York Times* best seller *Love Is the Killer App: How to Win Business and Influence Friends*. He is also the author of *The Likeability Factor* and *Saving the World at Work*, which was rated one of the Top 30 Business Books of 2008 by Soundview Executive, the leading reviewer of business books. Tim is a former executive at Yahoo!, where he served as chief solutions officer and also leadership coach. Today he is the CEO of Deeper Media, an online advice-content company. Tim has appeared on numerous television programs, including *The Today Show*, and has been featured in such publications as the *New York Times*, the *Wall Street Journal*, *Family Circle*, *Reader's Digest*, *Fast Company*, and *Businessweek*. Originally from New Mexico, Tim and his wife, Jacqueline, live in Los Angeles, California.

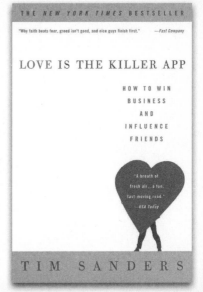